COVENT GARDEN

COVENT
GARDEN

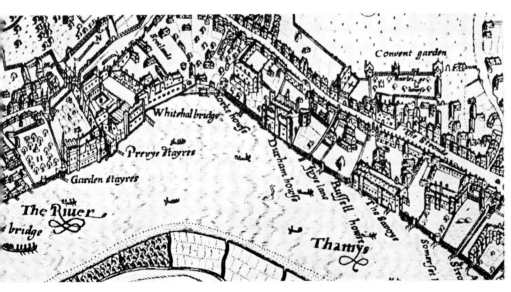

Photographs by A. F. Kersting F.R.P.S.

Text by Mary Cathcart Borer

Abelard-Schuman

LONDON   NEW YORK   TORONTO

Books written by Mary Cathcart Borer:

Mankind in The Making
Women Who Made History
The City of London
Famous Rogues
The People of Medieval England
The People of Tudor England

Text © Copyright Mary Cathcart Borer 1967

Photographs © Copyright Abelard-Schuman Ltd. 1967

First published 1967

Library of Congress Catalogue Card Number 67:19420

LONDON	NEW YORK	TORONTO
Abelard-Schuman Limited	Abelard-Schuman Limited	Abelard-Schuman Canada Limited
8 King Street WC2	6 West 57 Street	896 Queen Street West

ILLUSTRATIONS

Engravings

CONTENTS

ACKNOWLEDGMENTS

The author wishes to thank the Editor of THE ECONOMIST
for permission to reprint an extract from that journal.

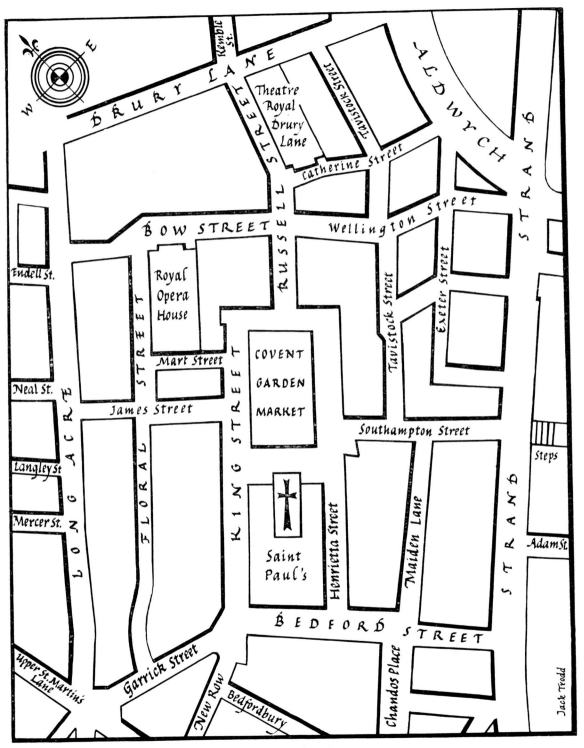

Covent Garden today.

Chapter 1
The Garden

SEVEN HUNDRED years ago, the road leading from the medieval, walled city of London to St. Peter's Abbey of Westminster, already known as the Strand, was a lonely, deeply-rutted, muddy track between the slow-flowing, marshy river Thames and the green fields of Middlesex. The abbots of Westminster owned a piece of land – seven acres of 'fair spreading pastures' – along the northern side of the highway, about half-way between the abbey and the city. Part of this land they used as a burial ground for their convent. Another area they cultivated as a kitchen garden, for their daily needs of fruit and vegetables. And as their gardeners grew more successful and enthusiastic, they sold their surplus products to the citizens of London, for the profit of their own foundation and the satisfaction of all.

Throughout the next 200 years, as the Plantagenet kings of England played out their violent destinies, the citizens of London grew wiser and their horizons widened. The city itself spread far beyond the confines of its Roman walls, to the east, the north and to the west, along the Strand towards Westminster. By the time of the Tudor Renaissance the south side of the Strand was lined with magnificent houses and palaces – Essex House, Arundel House, Somerset House, the Savoy Palace, Durham House, York House and Suffolk House – all of them set in tree-shaded gardens, with nobly conceived terraces and watersteps down to the river. Building had also begun amongst the fields and meadows of the northern side of the Strand and the convent garden and great field – the Long Acre – of the abbots of Westminster were enclosed within a brick wall. The produce of the

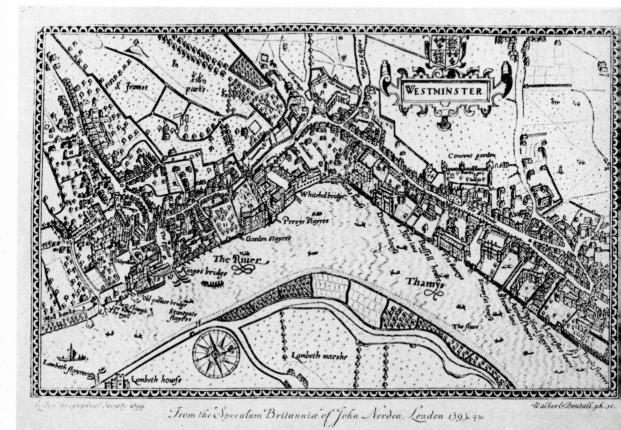

Covent Garden and surrounding areas in the late sixteenth century, according to Norden's Survey. The Garden and wall, the Long Acre or great field, and Burleigh House can clearly be seen.

garden was more popular than ever, for as the population of London steadily increased, the demand for fruit and vegetables grew each year.

With the Reformation, the lands of the Church became the property of the Crown and in due course were either sold or bestowed on favoured and useful noblemen. So it came about that, in 1552, Edward VI granted the garden, known as the Convent Garden and the Long Acre, to John Russell, Earl of Bedford; but this transfer of deeds in high places did not deter the people of London from continuing to obtain their fresh vegetables from their favourite source of supply. For many years to come, the Russell family did little to develop their seven acres, which was now part of the parish of St. Martin-in-the-Fields, but their gardeners still tended the orchard and vegetable plots and marketed their produce. Over the years people from neighbouring villages formed the habit of bringing their own wares to sell at the old Convent Garden, thereby creating for themselves an unauthorized but highly convenient market place. The rest of the seven acres the Russells let out to neighbouring members of the aristocracy for the stabling and pasturage of their horses, and a few small cottages were built there for the coachmen and ostlers, and also for the gardeners.

Facing the Strand, the Russells built their family mansion, Bedford House, 'with a great yard before it, for the reception of carriages; with a spacious garden, having a terraced walk adjoining the brick wall next to the garden, behind which were the coach houses and stables'. Also on the north side of the Strand, Lord Burleigh built Burleigh House during the reign of Queen Elizabeth I. Not far away, Sir William Drury had built his lovely Drury House, standing back a little from the Strand, in a lane which became known as Drury Lane, and when the Earl of Craven, love-sick for the widowed Queen of Bohemia, later moved into it, he rebuilt it and called it Craven House.

In 1630, during the reign of Charles I, the Russell family at last decided to lay out their inheritance of the Long Acre as a building site, for London was still growing fast and with it the demand for dwelling houses. The population of the country as a whole had increased to five and a half million, from the four million of a century earlier, and in London the population had doubled itself and was now approaching a quarter of a million.

The Russells chose for their architect the fashionable and distinguished Inigo Jones, who had studied his craft in Italy and had already designed the new Palace of Whitehall, with its lovely banqueting hall. Inigo Jones was producing work in the classical style of Greece and Rome. His buildings were dignified with pediments and pilasters, and his interiors had elegant staircases and beautifully proportioned rooms, often in the form of a double cube, made gracious with friezes and panels of moulding on the walls, ceilings of delightful Italian plaster work and marble floors.

He was commissioned to lay out the old Convent Garden as a square, surrounded by noble mansions, and to plan four streets to converge on it. He planned his square with tall, spacious houses, built with their first floors projecting over the pavements and supported by arches, to form covered pavement walks, in the manner of Italian piazzas. On the western side he designed a small church, for the future population of the new parish.

As the builders set to work and the plan took shape, the ancient fruit trees and the vegetable plots quickly disappeared. The northern and eastern piazzas began to rise. This was before the Great Fire, and Londoners, most of whom were still living in their small, half-timbered, deeply-eaved, crazily crooked houses, which had been standing since early Tudor times, had never seen anything like the piazzas before. They were enchanted. The church was built, with its dignified, pillared portico and its charmingly simple rose-red brick walls and large windows. But along the south side of the square the piazza was never built. Perhaps the Russells felt that they had invested enough money in their venture and should call a halt. Whatever the reason, for many years to come the tree-shaded garden wall of Bedford House served as the southern boundary. Moreover, Inigo Jones had been told to build his church simply and cheaply, so the Russell funds were probably beginning to run low. It soon became apparent that the church was the wrong way round, with the portico at its eastern end, but whether this was accidental or deliberate no one can now say with certainty. Anyway, the entrance on to the square, which is, of course, immediately behind the altar, was sealed and stood only for appearance's sake, and the main entrance, by way of the big west door, was built at the back, opening on to the little graveyard leading to the country lane which was soon to become Bedford Street.

The market people did not move. They assembled their wares under the garden wall of Bedford House and business flourished as never before, for more and more people came to watch the marvel of the new piazzas taking shape, and now there were also scores of workmen about – bricklayers and carpenters, glaziers and plasterers – as additional customers. Once the houses were completed, the Russell family had no trouble in finding tenants. Many members of the nobility chose houses in the piazzas for their town mansions, and the Convent Garden became a place of high fashion. Members of the new upper middle class followed them before long; the gentry and professional people, particularly the artists and writers. The building of the four streets leading to the square was soon under way. King Street led to the north-west corner. Henrietta Street, named after King Charles's queen, Henrietta Maria, ran to the south-west corner. James Street, called after the Duke of York, who later became the luckless James II, ran northwards to Long Acre, the original northern boundary of the site, where already the famous avenue of elm trees had been felled to make way for more new houses. Russell Street ran eastwards, cutting across yet another new street, Bow Street, 'being so built as running in the shape of a bent bow', which connected Russell Street with Long Acre, and on to the fast-developing Drury Lane.

By 1645 the Bedford development, by now vulgarized from the Convent Garden to Covent Garden, had become so populous, and so many new streets, including Bedford Street, were being built, that despite the protests of the incumbent of St. Martin-in-the-Fields, it was made into a separate parish and Inigo Jones's little church was dedicated to St. Paul.

14

Covent Garden and its environs in 1658, according to Hollar's map of London. In the space of half a century, the area has taken on much of its present shape. St. Paul's Church is built, as are the Piazzas on the north and east.

The troubled years of the Civil War were approaching. During this time and the eleven years of the Protectorate, all the inhabitants of Covent Garden, including the mercers and merchants, the wig-makers and tailors, the printers and bookbinders, the coach builders, the barbers, bakers and butchers, the fruit and vegetable mongers and the keepers of the innumerable taverns, who had crowded round to attend to the needs of the gentry, and were all living close at hand in the smaller houses of the Garden, lived soberly, with the outward decorum which expediency demanded. But the years of suppression did not last long. By 1660 Charles II was on the throne, and though Puritanism persisted and deepened in many other parts of the country, Covent Garden, by now deep set in the capital city, burst into new life again and became the very heart of the gay, vigorous Restoration mood.

Cromwell had ordered the closing down of the old Elizabethan and Jacobean theatres. These had been built decorously outside the City of London's boundaries, by order of the City fathers, but within easy walking distance: the Theatre, the Curtain, the Blackfriars Theatre, the Globe, the Rose, the Swan, the Fortune and the old Cockpit in Drury Lane, which later became the Phoenix. Here people had flocked to enjoy the plays of Shakespeare, Marlowe, Ben Jonson and the lesser dramatists, as well as all manner of entertainments, including cock-fights. Now Tom Killigrew, who was a friend of Charles II and had a passion for the drama, planned to build a new theatre and persuaded the King to issue a Royal Charter, which thereby helped to make the stage at last respectable. This charter also contained the important clause that henceforth women's parts, which before the Restoration had been played by men, could now be performed by women. Tom Killigrew built his Theatre Royal in Drury Lane, and for many years to come, till its rival, the Opera House, was built in Bow Street, it was known as the King's Theatre, or sometimes just the Covent Garden Theatre.

By 1662 the theatre was opened, and Covent Garden became more fashionable and populous than ever. Not only was the King himself fond of the play – and of all too many of the actresses – but playwrights and actors, good, bad and indifferent, arrived on the scene, for these were the days when everyone, of necessity, had to live close to his work. They came to frequent the taverns and newly-established coffee houses, to lodge in the streets surrounding the piazzas, to love and quarrel, to create and destroy, to reach the heights of acclaim and the depths of disappointment and despair, to triumph and suffer, and at the last to die and be buried in the Church of St. Paul.

In the aristocratic piazza itself, Sir Godfrey Kneller, Lord Brownlow, the Bishop of Durham, the Duke of Richmond, the Earl of Oxford, the Earl of Bedford, the Marquis of Windsor, the Earl of Sussex and the Earl of Peterborough

Covent Garden in 1660, looking west to St. Paul's Church. (Courtesy Covent Garden Market Authority.)

all had houses during these Restoration years. Of the Bishop, it was said that nearly all the foundlings left at the door of St. Paul's were laid at his door. This is a remarkably ambiguous statement, which must depend for its interpretation on the Christian charity of the reader.

Foremost of the Restoration dramatists was the gay and handsome William Wycherley, whose bawdy but brilliantly constructed comedies so vastly amused the new audiences. He lodged with his wife, the Countess of Drogheda, by the Cock Tavern in Bow Street; but the Countess, 'though a splendid wife, was not formed to make a husband happy'. In fact, she was so jealous of him that whenever he slipped into the Cock for a quiet drink, 'he was obliged to leave the windows open that his lady might see there was no woman in the company'. However, his

17

troubles came to an end in due course, for the Countess 'made him some amends by dying in a reasonable time'.

Dryden, the Poet Laureate, was the other great name writing for the new theatre. He lived in Long Acre but spent much of his time at Button's Coffee House in Russell Street, which also became a favourite haunt of Addison who always retreated there 'whenever he suffered any vexation' from his wife.

Pepys, who for some years was living nearby, in Buckingham Street south of the Strand, was frequently round and about Covent Garden during these gay years: but there were sad times too, for it was while walking down Drury Lane, on a June day in 1665, that he saw the first signs of the plague. 'This day much against my will I did in Drury Lane see two or three houses marked with a red cross upon the doors, and "Lord have mercy upon us" writ there; which was a sad sight to see, being the first of the kind that, to my remembrance, I ever saw,' he noted. The plague closed Drury Lane and all the other theatres of London for 18 months, and by the time they were re-opened the Great Fire had devastated much of the city to the east of Covent Garden, destroying a great deal that was good but also sweeping away many of the disease-ridden corners of its ancient, sunless alleys and courts. Inigo Jones had died in poverty only a few years after the death of Charles I, but a new young architect from Oxford, Christopher Wren, was called in to design the new City of London. And in unscarred Covent Garden a new star was growing to young womanhood, 'pretty, witty Nell', born in Coal Yard, Drury Lane, the daughter of a Covent Garden fruiterer. She began life as an orange seller in the King's Theatre, rose to be one of its leading actresses and then became a cherished mistress of King Charles II himself. Pepys was a great admirer of Nell Gwynne, and when he and his wife were introduced to her he was enraptured. She was, he said, 'a most pretty woman, who acted very fine . . . today. I kissed her, and so did my wife; and a mighty pretty soul she is.'

Pepys enjoyed himself greatly at the theatre that day, 'especially kissing of Nell'.

The market through which Pepys and Nell, Wycherley, Dryden and Tom Killigrew wandered and bargained and noted the procession of the seasons flourished and grew more popular than ever, so that, in 1671, Charles II granted the Earl of Bedford a licence for it. Like the theatre, Covent Garden market became respectable. The following year the theatre was burnt to the ground, but less than two years later Christopher Wren's new building had risen on the foundations of the old and Tom Killigrew was in business again.

In the market, 23 salesmen were registered and paying rates by 1680, but in appearance it had altered very little from the days when the piazzas were first built. Strype, in 1689, described it thus: 'The south side of Covent Garden Square lieth open to Bedford Garden, where there is a small grotto of trees, most pleasant in the summer season; and on this side there is kept a market for fruits, herbs, roots and flowers every Tuesday, Thursday and Saturday; which is grown to a considerable account, and well served with choice goods, which make it much resorted to.'

Charles II had died, rather young and unexpectedly. James II, after four troubled years, had abdicated, and William of Orange and Mary came to the throne, to be followed, in 1702, by Queen Anne. Times were changing ever more rapidly, as London continued to spread. To the north and west of Covent Garden there was more building, and some of the nobility began to move away to these even grander and larger new houses and squares. In 1704 the Russells moved from their old home to their new mansion in Bloomsbury, and old Bedford House was pulled down to make room for more streets of much smaller but still elegant dwelling houses. Tavistock Street was built and Southampton Street, where David Garrick was to live; and the famous Bedford Head, frequented by Pope and Walpole was established. Andrew Marvell made his home in Maiden Lane and so too for a spell did Voltaire – and Bedford Street was extended, where Quin and the Sheridan family lodged.

As the building of Covent Garden developed, there were created innumerable furtive alleyways and queer, dark little courtyards, leading between the larger houses, and in these were built mean and narrow dwellings for tradesmen in a small way of business, the poorer craftsmen and labourers. Into them now crowded a disreputable band of hangers-on, pick-pockets and prostitutes, tricksters and rogues. The audacious Jonathan Wild, who styled himself 'Thief-Taker General', was already operating from his house in the Old Bailey at this time. Apart from the activities of the highwaymen on the country roads around London, crime was rampant in the town itself, during the early years of the eighteenth century, and Covent Garden had its full share of the trouble.

Bow Street was running downhill fast and becoming the abode of habitual criminals when, in 1749, two of its distinguished residents, Sir John Fielding and his brother Henry, the novelist, both of them magistrates of Westminster, organized the Bow Street runners, to supplement the efforts of the aged and ineffectual 'night guardians' who hitherto had been the citizen's only protection against footpads, cut-throats and the like.

It was in 1737, during the reign of George II, that the first theatre in Bow Street was built, which was later to become known as the Royal Italian Opera House and where today stands the Royal Opera House, Covent Garden. More actors, writers, singers and musicians flocked to the Garden, and it reached the zenith of its affluence and gaiety. The market spread as the people prospered. By now it occupied almost the whole of the square, a large, gravelled space enclosed with posts and chains with a fine, fluted stone column surmounted by a sun dial in the middle, resting on a pedestal of six marble steps, on which old women sat to sell bowls of milk, porridge and broth. Through the market ladies of quality would walk from their homes in the piazzas or surrounding streets, black pages carrying their books, to daily prayer in the church of St. Paul. The covered booths where the fruit, flowers and vegetables were displayed were still little more than sheds, but the market people were proud to maintain the high standard of their wares. There were two herb shops, where you could buy leeches and snails – snail broth was strengthening for consumptives. There were all manner of hucksters and hawkers, including an itinerant bird-dealer, who sold larks, canaries and owls, and was open to receive orders for love birds and talking parrots. And there was Powel, the puppet man, who used the church bell as a signal for the opening of his own performance outside and continued the show throughout the service, thereby causing a lamentable decline in the numbers of St. Paul's congregations.

Wycherley and Dryden, Otway, Sir John Vanbrugh, Congreve, Thomas Betterton, Barton Booth and Macklin all had their day in Covent Garden. Sir Godfrey Kneller, Lely, Hogarth and Wilson lived and worked there. Steele and Addison were frequently to be found in its taverns and coffee houses, as well as Dr. Johnson, Boswell and Pope. During the eighteenth century, when Robert Adam and his brothers were building the Adelphi Terrace, Portland Place and Fitzroy Square, and Chippendale, Sheraton and Hepplewhite were designing their elegant furniture, the cultural life of London still centred on Covent Garden. David Garrick, before whom that grand old man of the theatre, Quin, had to give way, then Macklin, Mrs. Clive and Peg Woffington – all had their day, along with the musicians Gay, Handel and Arne. With a renewed interest in straight plays, Edmund Kean, Macready and Madame Vestris took the stage.

Unperturbed by it all, the market still flourished in their midst. In 1830 John, sixth Duke of Bedford, built the present market buildings, with a central arcade and two rows of shops, cut by another road running through at right angles. Rents and tolls for the shops were payable to the Duke, who had the power to make bye-laws for the good government of the market. In 1860 the flower market was opened. The Opera House was only just recovering from its second disastrous fire, and a few years later Chatterton was to launch his famous Drury Lane pantomimes. Henry Irving, a young actor of 22 at this time, was to give his last season at the Lane in the spring of 1905, and Ellen Terry, only 17 but already preparing to be a great actress, was to celebrate her stage jubilee there a few weeks later, in June of the same year.

Life in the Garden has been rich and deep. Poets and writers, actors, artists, musicians, dramatists and critics mingled there in true companionship. In the taverns and coffee houses they sharpened their wits and perfected their crafts. Despite the quarrels and jealousies, they came to understand and love each other and the market people on their doorsteps well, with the heightened perception and sensitivity which made them artists.

The Garden has known disasters and tragedies and constant change, but it has never died. Part of the eastern piazza was burnt down in 1796 and by 1896 it had completely gone. Drury Lane theatre was destroyed three times by fire and Covent Garden twice. St. Paul's Church was burnt and rebuilt. Taverns and coffee houses changed hands or closed down to make way for new establishments. Increasingly throughout the nineteenth century, merchants, tradesmen and people of the theatre who formerly had lived near their jobs moved away and travelled daily to their work in the Garden. In their deserted homes, slums and all their attendant vices developed, which in their turn have been cleared away.

Old actors grew feeble and lost their powers and went, in the end, to their burial at St. Paul's, but before the mourners had dried their tears new, young actors were walking the boards, to experience fresh triumphs and heartbreaks, disillusionments, compromises and contentments.

There are dozens of famous people buried in St. Paul's, and although most of the churchyard has gone, they and their work still live in the traditions of the great theatres they served. St. Paul's is still the actors' church, where many of the great men and women working in the theatre today will one day, inevitably, come to be remembered.

The market has spread relentlessly into the houses of the piazzas and the streets beyond. Some of its offices are housed in lovely Inigo Jones buildings, with majestic staircases. Now the market, over 700 years old, is bigger and more vigorous than it has ever been.

Although men of letters no longer live in the Garden, many publishing houses remain as their living memorial: Dent and Warne in Bedford Street, Country Life in Tavistock Street, Victor Gollancz and Duckworth in Henrietta Street, Newnes in Southampton Street and Odham's in Long Acre.

Drury Lane, the most famous theatre in the world, can also claim to have been used, in an unbroken continuity of 300 years, longer than any other threatre in Europe. The Opera House, with its present seasons of opera and ballet, is a vital part of our cultural life; and though 200 years old now, to each new generation it is a fresh and inspiring discovery.

Chapter 2
The Theatre Royal, Drury Lane

OLIVER CROMWELL'S Puritan government decreed that no theatrical performances should take place in England, but this was the kind of law which people who felt so inclined could usually manage to evade. Both Charles I and his Queen, Henrietta Maria, had been fond of the play, and Tom Killigrew, Page of Honour at the Court, had often entertained them with his own romantic pieces. During the years of the Commonwealth William Davenant, godson of Shakespeare and, some would have it, his natural son, surreptitiously staged plays at the old Cockpit in Drury Lane, though at a considerable risk both to the players and the audience. On at least one occasion Puritan soldiers broke in, cleared the auditorium, broke up the seats and the stage, confiscated all the props and costumes and locked up the players for a few days.

After a suitable interval, however, the company came together again, and it was at the Cockpit that the young Thomas Betterton received his early training and the handsome and charming Edward Kynaston continued the tradition of boys playing the women's parts.

With the Restoration, Killigrew and Davenant lost no time in talking to Charles II about the possibility of building new theatres in London. After much discussion they were granted a joint Royal Charter, which gave them a monopoly to build theatres and employ companies of actors. For a while, Killigrew and Davenant ran the old Cockpit together, but soon they parted. Davenant went to the old Duke's Theatre in Lincoln's Inn for a few years, but Killigrew leased a site from the Earl of Bedford, which lay at the corner of Drury Lane and what is now Catherine Street, in aristocratic and fashionable Covent Garden, in order to create the first Theatre Royal. He raised money for the building and collected his company of actors and actresses. They became members of His Majesty's Company of Comedians in Drury Lane and, as members of the King's Household, took an oath of allegiance to the King and were entitled to wear their own special livery.

The theatre was small – only about the size of the present stage at Drury Lane – but it was elegant and it housed 700 people. It had two tiers of boxes, including the splendid royal box, and a gallery. The floor of the theatre was occupied by a steeply ramped pit. The proscenium arch framed the stage, but there was a considerable projection of apron stage into the auditorium, as in the old Elizabethan theatres. There were windows, for the first performances were still held in daylight, but the stage was lit by candles suspended in chandeliers from the proscenium arch. Two generations later the first floats were used.

There was a curtain, and elaborately painted flats for scenery, which were an attractive innovation, but there was as yet very little stage furnishing, so that actors and actresses still tended to step forward on to the apron and declaim their parts, with the old formal gestures and movements.

Killigrew opened in May, 1663, with Beaumont and Fletcher's *The Humorous Lieutenant*, which Pepys thought 'a silly play', but which pleased the audience as a whole well enough. In the company were Charles Hart, a grand-nephew of Shakespeare, Michael Mohun and Edward Kynaston, all of whom were popular and talented. Killigrew's two leading ladies were the Marshall sisters, Anne and Beck, who reigned unchallenged till Nell appeared on the scene. Then the feathers flew. 'Nelly and Beck Marshall, falling out the other day,' reported Pepys, 'the latter called the other my Lord Buckhurst's whore. Nell answered then, "I was but one man's whore, though I was brought up in a bawdy-house to fill strong waters to the guests; and you are a whore to three or four, though a Presbyter's praying daughter!" which was very pretty.'

Things went fairly well at the Lane for the first few years, despite Killigrew's inevitable losses when the theatre had to close during the plague. He paid his way, and that says a good deal for the entertainment, for his audiences were a boisterous, rowdy, critical crowd, quick to acclaim but equally prompt to shout their disapproval when they were displeased.

At first, performances began at three in the afternoon. Gradually, as the candle and wax lighting improved, they took place later into the evening, though venturing out after dark was in itself a fairly hazardous undertaking in those days, with footpads, thieves and cut-throats lurking in the dark, twisting alleys and courts around the Lane. The people poured noisily into the theatre, pitting their wits against the sharks at the door who took their money, and found places for themselves in the pit or gallery. Then arrived the gentry, the fops and dandies, in their curled wigs and full-skirted coats, their satin waistcoats and full breeches, preening themselves in their boxes or even on the stage itself, to be better seen. With them came their wives and mistresses, in their long, hooped skirts and low cut bodices, their powdered curls and swirling cloaks, decorously masked as time went on and the Restoration comedies became ever bawdier and more outrageous. The masks were to hide their blushes, they said, but they also established an anonymity which, at times, was useful both to themselves and their escorts. And Mary Meggs – Orange Moll – bought the concession for her girls to sell oranges, lemons and sweetmeats – as well, no doubt, as other favours – to the pit and boxes.

Killigrew staged Dryden, Ben Jonson and, in 1671, the Duke of Buckingham's satire, *The Rehearsal*. That was the year when Davenant's widow and sons opened the long-awaited new theatre in Dorset Fields at Greyfriars, down by the river off Fleet Street. It was a beautiful house, designed by Christopher Wren, with the newest ideas in lighting and stage equipment, and the company was headed by Thomas Betterton, who was reaching the peak of his great powers. People flocked to see him and Killigrew's audiences began to dwindle.

Betterton was undoubtedly the finest actor of his time. 'It's beyond imagination,' whispered Pepys to his companion, while watching Betterton's Hamlet. 'Mr. Betterton is the best actor in the world.'

Though no one had yet thought of stage costume, and players still appeared, for all parts and periods, in their everyday wigs, coats and breeches, Betterton had developed his own acting technique since the days of his early training at the Cockpit. 'When you speak of yourself,' he said, 'the right, not the left hand, must be applied to the bosom . . . but this action, generally speaking, should be only applied or expressed by laying the hand gently on the breast and not by thumping it as some people do. The gesture must pass from the left to the right and there end in gentleness and moderation.'

Betterton's style must have been a welcome contrast to the ranting performances, the strutting and roaring of the earlier tragedians. His restraint, far from diminishing his power, enhanced it, for Barton Booth, that other distinguished actor of the Restoration theatre, acting the Ghost to Betterton's Hamlet, confessed that 'instead of aweing him, he terrified me. But divinity hung around that man.'

Nell had left Killigrew to be with the King, and now came fresh disaster. In January 1672, after the play was over and everyone had gone home, fire broke out in Orange Moll's store room and spread with relentless speed. The brave new Theatre Royal was totally destroyed.

Tom Killigrew's first concern was for the livelihood of his company. He moved them to the old Duke's Theatre in Lincoln's Inn and then set about raising money for rebuilding of Drury Lane. This time he, too, employed Christopher Wren and planned a much bigger theatre, which would house 2,000 people.

Again it had an apron stage, but funds were low and the theatre had to be very plain, compared with the grandeur of the first one. He opened in March, 1674 with another play of Beaumont and Fletcher, this time *The Beggar's Bush*. The opening night was a success, but the good times did not last and the Duke's Theatre in Dorset Fields for a long time remained more popular. As audiences dwindled, so did the salaries of the actors, and more and more of them, including Anne Marshall, deserted to the Davenants' theatre.

Killigrew and several of his original company were growing old and tired. Killigrew retired, handing his patent to his two sons, but neither Charles nor Henry had Tom's flair for the theatre. They mismanaged badly, and matters went steadily downhill. They blamed the popularity of the Duke's Theatre for their misfortunes, but this was not entirely true, for there seems to have been a bad slump in theatre business early in the 1680s and their rivals were running into trouble too. By the end of 1682 they had solved the problem by amalgamating, and with Thomas Betterton as the leading actor and the Davenant brothers in management, Drury Lane seemed set for a revival of her fortunes.

The cast was the most talented and distinguished that the theatre had ever had, and now the piazzas and streets, the coffee houses and taverns of Covent Garden were to know such great names as the Mountforts, the Leighs, Mrs. Bracegirdle and Mrs. Barry, as well as the best of the old Drury Lane company, particularly Edward Kynaston.

The fine new theatre in Dorset Fields became tarnished and neglected. It was bought by Christopher Rich, but did not survive long and was finally pulled down. Drury Lane was supreme once more, the only theatre with a royal patent.

The manners and modes of the times were licentious and crude, and the plays which the Davenants now presented at the Lane were well matched to them – the works of Dryden, Wycherley, Sedley, Otway, Etherege and Shadwell; though such artists as Betterton and his leading ladies seemed to rise above the lewdness and communicate the essential drama of the plays.

However, the Davenants were no better managers than the Killigrew brothers had been. It was not long before they sold their patent to Christopher Rich, a cheese-paring old skinflint who remained at the Lane for the next ten years, despite quarrels and dissension amongst his company.

More famous names were coming to the fore. One day in 1692 there arrived at Drury Lane a young man called William Congreve. He persuaded Rich and Betterton to read a play he had just written – *The Old Bachelor* – and when they

25

presented it, a few months later, it was a resounding success. Congreve followed it with *The Double Dealer*, and then, one day, Kynaston being too ill to play his role of Lord Touchwood, a raw understudy, little dreaming of the heights to which fortune would one day bring him, stepped into the part. He was Colley Cibber.

But behind the scenes resentment against Christopher Rich was growing. Salaries were not only low, but irregular. At last Betterton appealed to King William and obtained permission for a licence to re-open the old theatre in Lincoln's Inn. Many of his colleagues went with him and so did the young Congreve, writing *Love for Love* for their opening night. Cibber remained with Rich, and for the next few years the rivalry between the two theatres was intense. Cibber was no great actor, but he gained real success when he wrote and acted in his own play, *Love's Last Shift:* and when Sir John Vanbrugh wrote a sequel to it, *The Relapse* or *Virtue in Danger*, the Lane was on its feet again. Their luck held for a while, for George Farquhar wrote *Love and a Bottle* and *The Constant Couple* for them. They found another rising star in Robert Wilks, and Doggett, the popular comedian, came over to them from Lincoln's Inn.

By the end of the seventeenth century, however, stagnation was descending on the English theatre. Dryden had written his last play in 1675. Wycherley had sunk into debt and decay and was spending time in the Fleet prison. Etherege was dead. In dire poverty poor Otway had died, in 1685, when he was only 33, of drink and a broken heart from a hopeless, unrequited love for Mrs. Barry. Congreve never wrote another play after *The Way of the World*, produced at Lincoln's Inn in 1700, but spent the next 27 years of his life basking in the honours he had won as a literary wit and enjoying life with his mistress, the Duchess of Marlborough, who, at the appointed time, gave him a magnificent funeral in Westminster Abbey.

In 1698 Jeremy Collier published his *Short View of the Immorality of the English Stage*, which was a protest against the obscenity, profanity and immorality of the plays which had been appearing in London. Congreve and Vanbrugh tried to justify themselves, but Dryden admitted that 'in many things he has taxed me justly'. Most people agreed with Collier, and the taste for Restoration drama declined. In its place, Italian opera began to have a vogue, together with spectacular shows of jugglers, conjurers, acrobats and the like.

Sir John Vanbrugh designed and opened a small theatre in the Haymarket for opera, in 1705, and when the first venture failed, the company at Lincoln's Inn joined him there for a while, to present straight plays. Rich continued to pay his way at the Lane by putting on, to the indignation of the true actors in his company, any form of entertainment which might bring in money, but it was through his dishonesty over money matters that he was at last ousted. Colley Cibber, Doggett and Wilks formed a joint actor-management of Drury Lane. Vanbrugh pulled out of the Haymarket. It was taken over solely for opera again, while Rich retreated to the Lincoln's Inn theatre, which he set about rebuilding.

That grand old actor, Betterton, was failing in health and in 1710 he died, but his pupil, Barton Booth, now rose to fame at Drury Lane, and before long had replaced Doggett as one of the three actor managers. His first great triumph came when he played the name part in Addison's new play, *Cato*.

Nevertheless, the art of acting was developing very slowly. Actors, in their periwigs and full coats, still used the old formalized gestures and declaimed their speeches from the apron, and it was perhaps small wonder that operas and musicals became increasingly popular in London and that Rich prospered at Lincoln's Inn Fields. When he died, his son John took over, and made a fortune from *The Beggar's Opera*, which Gay offered him in 1726. With the proceeds, John Rich bought a site in Bow Street and built his new Theatre Royal in Covent Garden, which for many years to come was to be a thorn in the flesh of Drury Lane. It opened in 1732, with a revival of Congreve's *The Way of The World*, and here James Quin grew to fame as the foremost actor of his time.

At the Lane, Barton Booth died the next year. Two years later, the lovely Anne Oldfield, one of their brightest stars, was dead. Another two years passed and Wilks was carried to his burial in St. Paul's, Covent Garden. Then the elegant and accomplished Colley Cibber retired, though he was to live on till 1757. Drury Lane was under a cloud. Rich's new theatre, almost on their doorstep, did not help matters, and now there was cause for further concern. George II had appointed Handel as Court musician, and a new, successful theatre had opened in the Haymarket, devoted largely to the performance of Handel's music and operas.

With the retirement of Cibber, the management of Drury Lane had come, after several manoeuvres, into the hands of Charles Fleetwood. Amongst his company was a young actress, Kitty Clive, and a hot-tempered young Irishman, Charles Macklin, as well as James Quin, who had come over from Covent Garden. Though James Quin was considered to be the finest actor on the London stage, and a worthy successor to Barton Booth, his acting was still in the old tradition, with speeches declaimed in grave sonority, deep and rich, if somewhat monotonous. It was Macklin who at last broke away from the old, mannered interpretations and established a new conception of the actor's true function.

He first showed his originality with a new portrayal of Shylock, a part which hitherto had always been played by the low comedian, who had contrived to turn him into a figure of fun. Macklin for the first time portrayed Shylock as

27

pathetic and even, in the end, tragic: and as Pope neatly observed afterwards:

This is the Jew
That Shakespeare drew.

The warm-hearted but temperamental Kitty Clive played Portia to Macklin's Shylock. The other star actress at the Lane was Mrs. Pritchard, famous for her Lady Macbeth, for which she wore, like all tragediennes, long black gloves with her eighteenth-century Court dress.

In 1742 the young David Garrick arrived at Drury Lane, having come to London from Lichfield a few years earlier with his friend Samuel Johnson. So now at the Lane were Quin, Macklin, Garrick, Mrs. Clive and Mrs. Pritchard. Macklin was soon outshining Quin, and before long, to the consternation of them both, Garrick was far ahead of either of them. They protested at his restlessness, his pace, his new ways on the stage, but his power over the audience was undeniable. 'If this young fellow be right, then *we* have all been wrong,' admitted Quin at last. Within five years, Garrick was jointly managing Drury Lane, and he was to rule there for nearly 30 years, till 1776.

Garrick's style was different from anything that had ever been seen on the stage before. He was short for a tragedian, for he was only five feet four inches and always wore very high shoes, but he moved well and had an extremely expressive face. His aim, like Macklin's, was to free acting from the restraints which long tradition had imposed, particularly in the interpretation of classical roles, but he went much farther and deeper than the older actor. He studied his characters with a clear, fresh mind and with sympathy and understanding, identifying himself with them, suffering their pain and tragedies, living in their emotions of joy and love, agony, fear and remorse. He had the gift of empathy, which involves both the emotions and the intellect, and was able, through a keen observation of the world around him, to take on the very essence of the personalities of his parts. This was the secret of Garrick's genius and the reason that he was acclaimed as greater even than Betterton.

Describing a performance of *The Fair Penitent*, a contemporary writer said that Quin appeared as Horatio, wearing an enormous periwig, rolled stockings and high-heeled, square-toed shoes, and that he spoke in 'deep, full tones, with little variation in cadence, accompanied by a sawing kind of action which had more of the senate than of the stage in it, rolling out heroics with an air of dignified indifference'. Mrs. Cibber, as Calista, spoke in a voice which was 'so extremely wanting in contrast, that though it did not wound the ear, it wearied it', but 'when little Garrick bounced on the stage it seemed as if a whole century had been swept over in the transition of a single scene; old things were done away and a new order at once brought forward, bright and luminous, and clearly destined to dispel the barbarisms and bigotry of a tasteless age, too long attached to the prejudices of custom and superstitiously devoted to the illusions of imposing declamation'.

For all his artistry, Garrick did not yet adopt realism in stage costume, declaring that the audiences would never accept it. He played Lear in eighteenth-century breeches, white shirt and ermine-trimmed coat and Macbeth in a full court suit, embroidered with gold. But he was an all-round man of the theatre and as convincing in comedy as in tragedy.

Peg Woffington, who first appeared at Covent Garden, came to play at Drury Lane from time to time and was, for a while, Macklin's mistress. Then she fell in love with Garrick. At one period, all three lived together, at a house in Bow Street. Then Macklin departed and eventually Garrick and Peg quarrelled and parted, on account of Peg's hopeless extravagance. Macklin left the stage altogether for a while and opened a public ordinary in Covent Garden Square, but the venture failed and he was very soon back at the Lane.

Mrs. Cibber, Colley Cibber's daughter-in-law, became one of the Lane's famous actresses. She had begun her stage career as a singer and Handel had been a great admirer of her voice. He had written the part of Galatea for her in his serenade, *Acis and Galatea*, and also some of the arias in *The Messiah*, but she wearied of opera and oratorio and came to Drury Lane to act with Garrick.

Garrick served the theatre well. He brought order to the stage and cleared away the stage boxes, so that the actors had it to themselves. He made many practical improvements, particularly in regard to lighting, and appointed Dr. Arne as musical director. He insisted on regular, punctual rehearsals and inspired his players with his own spirit of naturalism in acting, so that Drury Lane now became a theatre where people came not so much to see the play as to enjoy the acting.

It was Garrick who introduced the first Drury Lane pantomime, and at last he began the dress reforms which were later to develop into stage realism. He married very happily and lived for many years in Southampton Street, but when Peg Woffington was suffering from her last illness he did not forget her and was kind. A few years later, in 1766, both Quin and Mrs. Cibber died. Shortly afterwards Kitty Clive retired to Strawberry Hill, where she lived for many more years, enjoying the company of her friend Walpole's literary circle, but the ageing Macklin hung on in the theatre for years. His last performance was not till 1789, by which time he was said to be well advanced into the nineties, and his power and his memory had all gone, but even then he lived on for another ten years, in his lodgings in Covent Garden, pottering about the piazzas and haunting the theatre which had been the scene of his life's achievements.

It was in 1776 that the brilliant but erratic Richard Sheridan arrived at Drury Lane, having written *The Rivals* when he was only 24. Garrick was growing old and needed a rest. He retired and Sheridan, with two associates, took over the patent of Drury Lane. *The Rivals* and *The School For Scandal* were both glittering successes, but Sheridan had no head for business and the financial affairs of the theatre soon became hopelessly mismanaged. Garrick came back from time to time to help with rehearsals, but only three years later he died.

Sheridan struggled on. At his Christmas pantomimes the little clown, Jo Grimaldi, first appeared and soon became an institution and a constant source of delight. Among Sheridan's outstanding players was Robert Baddeley, the last of the Drury Lane players to wear the royal livery off-stage; then, in 1782, came Sarah Siddons, whose first appearance at the Lane some years earlier had been a failure. She had gained experience in the provinces and had time to learn her craft well. Now, in the supreme testing-place of Drury Lane, she was an unqualified success, proving herself to be one of the most compelling tragediennes the theatre had ever known. The whole of fashionable London came to see her. She was an individualist, as Garrick had been, and despite Sheridan's urgent protests, she insisted on deviating from Mrs. Pritchard's long established interpretation of Lady Macbeth in the sleep-walking scene. She set down the candle and wrung her hands in true anguish, so painful that James Sheridan Knowles, playing opposite her, declared afterwards: 'I smelt blood! I swear I smelt blood!'

She was an extremely beautiful woman, but so great were her powers of empathy that she could make herself look utterly worn and emaciated, where the part called for it. Her eyes would become lustreless and not only her voice but her whole body seemed to undergo a physcial change. The spell-bound audience was moved to tears by her pathos.

Mrs. Siddons introduced her brother, John Kemble, to the Lane. Though he did not possess his sister's genius, he was a tall and impressive figure and his acting was dignified and restrained. His style was different from Garrick's – more classical and less naturalistic – but he brought intelligence and sympathy to his interpretations and he soon become Sheridan's leading man and manager.

Despite financial worries, Kemble restored something of the old orderliness which had ruled in Garrick's time, but by 1791 it was all too apparent that the theatre, by now 117 years old, was becoming extremely dilapidated and unsafe. It was condemned, and Sheridan had to set about raising the money for a new building. The second Theatre Royal was pulled down almost entirely, though Wren's foundations were left and still exist. The company moved to the Hay-

Auditorium of the Theatre Royal, burned down in February 1809.

market theatre while Holland built the third Drury Lane. It opened in 1794 with a lavish production of Macbeth, in which both Sarah Siddons and John Kemble appeared.

Throughout the next few years no better acting could be found anywhere in the country than at the Lane, but all was not well behind the scenes. Sheridan, always short of money, was in debt all round, and at last, in 1805, Mrs. Siddons and John Kemble, both owed arrears of salary, could stay no longer. They departed to Covent Garden. Sheridan had lost his two most valuable players, but an even greater disaster was awaiting him. In 1809 fire broke out in the theatre and

31

once more it was burned to the ground. The third Drury Lane had cost over £250,000, but it was insured for only £35,000. As Sheridan sat watching the blazing theatre, from the Piazza coffee house in Covent Garden Square, he knew that he was ruined.

With infinite courage he set about organizing funds for the rebuilding. The money was forthcoming without much difficulty, for people were sympathetic and generous, but he was never again to be the lessee. The fourth and present theatre, built by Benjamin Wyatt, opened in 1812, in the middle of the Napoleonic wars, though the portico and colonnade were added several years later. Garrick survived the disaster by only four years, and Samuel Arnold became the new licensee.

With the new theatre, a new actor, perhaps the finest of them all, appeared at the Lane – the turbulent, brilliant Edmund Kean. He arrived in 1814, a young man of 27, shabby, poverty-striken and already embittered, for his wife and child were half starving and his elder boy had died because they had been too poor to give him the care he needed. The rest of the players at first ignored the forlorn-looking newcomer, who had somehow managed to be given the important part

The new Theatre Royal, opened in 1812.

of Shylock for his first appearance, but when he put on a black wig and beard they eyed him askance. Even Macklin had respected tradition sufficiently to wear the customary red wig. Standing aloof from them all, Kean waited in the wings. His cue came and he made his entrance. From the first moment, he held not only his audience but the rest of the players with the power of his acting. His conquest of the Drury Lane stage was unquestioned, and everyone knew that here was an actor greater even than Kemble, still reigning supreme across the way at Covent Garden. From that first night Kean was the leader of his profession. 'By God, he is a soul!' exclaimed Lord Byron, after seeing his Othello.

But Kean's early, tragic struggles had weakened him. He could not take success. He drank heavily and became arrogant and truculent. Despite increasing success on the stage, he wasted his vitality and incomparable talents in the lowest taverns around Covent Garden, drinking and brawling and more than once ending up in Bow Street for the night. Before many years had passed came the time when he was too drunk to appear. Though he missed that performance, he was forgiven, for he was still a superb actor and paid little account to the younger generation of actors growing up round him, learning their profession and eager for their own, brief triumphs.

The Lane was badly in debt again. The committee who had been acting as lessees with Arnold resigned in 1819. The new lessee was Robert Elliston, who put on some lavishly staged Shakespearean productions for Kean, but shortly afterwards Kean departed for America.

Playwriting as an art was in decline in England. Few people were writing seriously for the stage, for the taste in entertainment had turned to musicals, shows, spectaculars and melodrama. Nevertheless, when Kean came back to England, Elliston billed him for a new Shakespeare season. Not only was Kean drinking more heavily than ever, but he had become involved in an affair with Charlotte Cox, the wife of a City alderman, who brought an action against him. Kean became the centre of a titillating scandal. He lost the case and Charlotte left him for another lover. He attempted a come-back and overcame the initial hostility of the audience, but drink had sapped his power and ruined his memory and concentration. Before the rising star of a new young actor, William Macready, the great Ned Kean, though occasionally summoning his old magic with such determination that it seemed as though he were truly recovering, gradually ran downhill. When his son, Charles, told him that he was going to be an actor, too, Ned quarrelled with him bitterly. The sight of the boy's youth and untried strength, his enthusiasm and fresh enchantment with the theatre, must have brought him the sharpest anguish of regret for his own destroyed talents, but in the end they were reconciled. Charles made his first appearance at the Lane in 1827

B

and four years later his father died, at the age of 46. Poor little Grimaldi was dead too. He had long been crippled and unable to clown, and all his money was gone. In June of 1828 they carried him on to the stage. From a chair he performed for the last time, for his 'benefit', and he still had the power to make his audience laugh.

The Lane had a chequered career for the next few years, presenting a heterogeneous collection of entertainments, musicals, spectaculars, operas, and plays of no great merit. For a time Alfred Bunn was in control, but in 1841 Macready, by this time the greatest tragedian of the English stage and friend of Charles Dickens, Landseer, Bulwer Lytton and many other members of literary and artistic London circles, took over the theatre for a while, opening with a production of *The Merchant of Venice*.

Times were changing very quickly in England now, for the railway age had begun. More people were living in London or coming in from the ever-growing suburbs, demanding entertainment. They were not particularly discriminating, and wanted amusement rather than intellectual stimulus. More theatres were opening and competition for customers was keen.

Macready, great artist as he was, did not fill the house. He raised the prestige of Drury Lane as the home of true drama, but two years later he found that he had lost £20,000 in the venture and pulled out. Alfred Bunn returned, with Charles Kean, who by now had risen to stardom and appeared as Richard II. The production was splendidly lavish, and it was Charles who first achieved true historical accuracy on the stage, for both costumes and sets; but Bunn made more money from a brand new opera he now offered to his public. It was Balfe's *The Bohemian Girl*.

The year of London's Great Exhibition, in 1851, saw the retirement of the great Macready. During the next few years there was a succession of famous actor-managers at the Lane, who were to win great honours but also lose most of their money. By 1866 the kindly and generous F. B. Chatterton was in command, and it was he who staged the extravagantly spectacular and realistic pantomimes and melodramas which so delighted the Victorian public. Even so, seventeen years later he was bankrupt, and he lived only long enough to see the young Augustus Harris in his place. Harris remained at the Lane till his tragically early death in 1896, offering everything that seemed to have possibilities for entertainment: Shakespeare, light opera, grand opera, drama and even nigger minstrel shows, as well as the Christmas pantomime, for which he engaged many musical hall artists to add to the attractions – Vesta Tilley, Kate Vaughan, Fred Storey, Dan Leno, Marie Lloyd and a host of others.

In 1896 there was a serious threat to the Lane. Covent Garden market was spreading fast. There was a suggestion that the Duke of Bedford might not renew the lease, and that the theatre might be pulled down and the site handed over to the market. Disaster was averted, however, and Arthur Collins, who had arrived as a scene painter and emerged as an actor, now formed a limited liability company for Drury Lane, with himself as managing director. He obtained a new 80-year lease after the end of the one which might have been the last. Here he continued, in the Harris tradition, until 1924, with bigger and more realistic spectaculars than ever before, and more lavish and even longer pantomimes.

In the latter part of the nineteenth century serious dramatists were writing again, but their plays were not shown at the Lane. Tom Robertson had begun the cult of the new drama of social realism with *Caste*. Pinero was writing and Ibsen's plays had reached London. Bernard Shaw was climbing to success. At the same time, the art of the actor was changing, for it was now his task to portray the contemporary manners of the new plays, and inevitably his acting changed from the old flourish of over-elaborate gestures and exaggerated reactions to a more restrained, even casual style.

Collins clung for the most part to his melodramas and musicals, though Sir Henry Irving did a few Shakespeare seasons at Drury Lane and so did Ellen Terry. In 1913 Sir Johnston Forbes-Robertson gave his closing season there, opening and ending with Hamlet, while in 1916 Sir Frank Benson was there for the tercentenary celebrations of Shakespeare's birth.

For a while, during the First World War, Drury Lane became a cinema, showing Griffith's two epic films *The Birth of a Nation* and *Intolerance*, but by 1920 the old playhouse was back to normal, with Godfrey Tearle and Madge Titheradge appearing in *The Garden of Allah*. In 1922 the inside of the great theatre had a complete overhaul and soon afterwards, in 1924, Collins retired and Sir Alfred Butt took over.

Sir Alfred launched a succession of highly successful musicals – *Rose Marie*, *The Desert Song*, *Show Boat*, *The New Moon*, *The Three Musketeers* and *The Song of The Drum*. The big event of the Christmas holidays was always the Julian Wylie pantomime. In 1931 George Grossmith presented Richard Tauber in *The Land of Smiles* and then Charles Cochran put on Noël Coward's *Cavalcade*.

Ivor Novello's musicals began their long run of success in 1933, with *Glamorous Nights*, followed by *Careless Rapture*, *Crest of the Wave* and *The Dancing Years*. That brings us to September, 1939 and the outbreak of the Second European War, when all the theatres and cinemas of London were closed for a while.

But Drury Lane re-opened a week or two later, not to present a show but as the headquarters of ENSA. Mrs. Siddon's dressing room, Garrick's room, the Green room where Macklin, in a backstage quarrel, had accidentally killed a fellow player, all became offices organizing shows for the Forces at home and abroad, and the Drury Lane ghost which still haunts the old theatre in his long grey cloak, powdered wig and elegant tricorn hat, must have been perplexed and troubled.

The theatre was severely damaged by enemy bombing but miraculously escaped destruction. As soon as the war was over and ENSA had been disbanded, repairs were put in hand. By December, 1947, the Lane was ready for another first night – Noël Coward's *Pacific, 1860* – and once again a happy, expectant audience streamed into the beautiful theatre, through the vestibule with its cenotaph and long record of past patent holders, into the rotunda, with its statues of Shakespeare, Garrick, Kean and Balfe, and up the great staircase and into the grand circle, with their portraits and busts of the men and women who have made its history.

In 1947 began the series of brilliantly successful musicals by Richard Rodgers and Oscar Hammerstein II, *Oklahoma, Carousel, South Pacific* and *The King and I.* In April, 1958, the long-awaited *My Fair Lady* opened its record-breaking, five year run and then, in 1964, came *Camelot.*

The theatre which began 300 years ago and has seen so much history and romance, disaster and tragedy, triumph and achievement has never been more popular and successful than it is today, and every actor and actress worth his salt still dreams of one day playing the Lane.

Chapter 3
The Opera House

IT WAS on December 7, 1732, that John Rich opened his splendid new theatre. It was grander and more luxurious than any that London had ever seen before, and for many years to come was to present both plays and operas. Rich used Davenant's royal patent, which had been granted by Charles II, but that king had been dead for nearly half a century by now, the Stuarts had long been in exile, and on the throne of England reigned the German George II. There was still a monopoly on the running of theatres in England, though it was not rigidly observed. Nevertheless, it was not till early in the nineteenth century, when the patent law was ended, that people were legally free to open theatres for any kind of entertainment they wished.

Rich's theatre, with its pillared portico and beautiful Amiconi ceiling, was designed by James Shepherd. Its seating capacity was similar to that of Drury Lane – about 2,000 – and a full house would have been worth about £200. The main entrance was in Bow Street, but there was also an entrance by way of the eastern piazza in Covent Garden Square, which meant that among the people of the crowded market place – the greengrocers and flower sellers, the huddle of hucksters, the tavern keepers, the proprietors of the coffee houses, the quack doctors and fortune tellers, the panders and prostitutes – came ever more players and their admirers. For the market people business flourished as never before, whatever the varying fortunes of the theatres might be.

For John Rich, whose father had been so ignominiously turned out of Drury Lane, the return to Covent Garden was a triumph which he thoroughly enjoyed,

'Rich's Glory' by William Hogarth. John Rich opens his splendid new theatre, December 7, 1732.

and Hogarth's cartoon, *Rich's Glory*, shows his exultant arrival from Lincoln's Inn Fields. From the outset, the shows he staged were more spectacular and lavish than those at Drury Lane, particularly the pantomimes, for which John Rich, himself an actor of no mean talents, had created the part of Harlequin. It, was here in his new theatre, in association with George Lambert the scene painter, that he founded the famous Beefsteak Club.

At the Haymarket, Handel had been running into trouble with the management, so he joined Rich, who alternated his presentation of plays with operas and ballets. Handel's *Ariodante* and *Alcina* both had their *premières* at Covent Garden during the 1730s, and amongst his singers were Rich's son-in-law, John Beard, and Cecilia Young, who was to marry Thomas Arne, as well as Giovanni Carestini the male contralto and Maria Negri the soprano.

In 1736 Handel presented three new oratorios, *Alexander's Feast*, *Acis and Galatea* and *Esther*, all of which were triumphantly successful. For these, as for his operas, admission charges were raised. Writing of the performance of *Alexander's Feast*, *The Daily Post* reported[1]: 'There never was, upon the like occasion, so numerous and splendid audiences at any theatre in London, there being at least 1,300 persons present, and it is judged that the receipts of the House could not amount to less than £450.' During Lent, Covent Garden gave concerts of sacred music, for which Handel composed his sacred oratorios *Samson*, *Judas Maccabaeus* and *Solomon;* and then, in 1741, came the greatest of them all, *The Messiah*.

In the early years, John Rich's star actor was Quin, and he very soon found the young Peg Woffington, who first appeared at Covent Garden in 1738, beginning a brilliant but tempestuous stage career of nearly 20 years. One of her bitterest rivals was the beautiful George Anne Bellamy, and the charming Bellamy, we are told[2], had on one occasion, 'procured from Paris two gorgeous dresses wherein to enact Statira in *The Rival Queens*. Roxana was played by Woffington, and she was so overcome by malice when she saw herself eclipsed by the dazzling glories of the resplendent Bellamy, that she rolled Statira and her spangled sack in the dust, pommelling her the while with the handle of her stage dagger, as she declaimed, Alexander standing by:

'"Nor he, nor heaven shall shield thee from my justice!
Die, sorceress, die! and all my wrongs die with thee!"'

With the passing years, new stars arose to rival Quin, first Macklin and then Garrick, who came over from the Lane to appear at Covent Garden in 1746. And it was here, only eleven years later, that poor Peg Woffington, while playing

[1] Quoted in *Two Centuries of Opera at Covent Garden* by Harold Rosenthal.
[2] *Old and New London*, by Edward Walford.

her favourite part of Rosalind in *As You Like it*, suddenly collapsed with a stroke, and was carried off the stage, never to return.

Garrick had employed Arne as musical director at Drury Lane, but in 1760 Arne moved to Covent Garden. The following year Rich died and his son-in-law, John Beard, the tenor, took over the management for the production of Arne's lyric operas, of which the best known now are *Thomas and Sally*, *Artaxerxes* and *Love in a Village*.

Despite the elegance of the theatre and the quality of the presentations, the eighteenth century gallery audiences were as boisterous at Covent Garden as at the Lane. A visiting Frenchman reported in 1763 that there was 'a great deal of barking and howling and throwing of orange peel at a man whose face displeased the gallery. The gallery controlled the acting and thanked the players.'3

When *Artaxerxes* was presented, the production was so costly that the management decided to raise admission prices, but the audience, less docile than the modern British public, not only objected strongly but showed their resentment in no uncertain manner: 'A riot happened at Covent Garden theatre occasioned by a demand being made for full prices at the opera of *Artaxerxes*. The mischief done was the greatest ever known on any occasion of the like kind; all the benches of the boxes and pit being entirely torn up, the glasses and chandeliers broken, and the linings of the boxes cut to pieces. The rashness of the rioters was so great that they cut away the wooden pillars between the boxes, so that if the inside of them had not been iron, they would have brought the galleries down upon their heads. The damages done amount to at least £2,000. Four persons concern'd in the riots have been committed to the Gatehouse.'

In London new playwrights were at work. In 1768 Oliver Goldsmith's *The Good-Natured Man* was presented at Covent Garden and five years later *She Stoops to Conquer*, but by this time Beard had sold his patent, and, after a year or two of manoeuvring, Thomas Harris had become sole manager of the theatre. A year or two later, young Sheridan arrived in London, and his first play, *The Rivals*, was produced at Covent Garden, before he joined Garrick at the Lane the following year.

Interspersed with the plays, Harris now presented Italian operas by Piccinni, Tarchi, Paisiello and other contemporary Italian composers, in which one of the notable performers was Luigi Marchesi, the male soprano. After a performance of Tarchi's *La Generosita d'Alessandro*, the *Morning Post* reported that Marchesi had never sung to better effect, but 'the leading soprano, Giuliani, was chiefly distinguished for the very disgusting mode of rolling her eyes and distorting her features.'4

3Quoted in *Two Centuries of Opera at Covent Garden*, by Harold Rosenthal.
4Quoted in *Two Centuries of Opera at Covent Garden*, by Harold Rosenthal.

The first performance of *Aladdin* as a pantomime was in 1788, and the next year Charles Macklin, old and feeble and long past the effort, attempted to play his famous role of Shylock for his benefit, but he forgot his lines, broke down and had to be led from the stage.

When, some years later, Mrs. Siddons and John Kemble left Sheridan at the Lane and went to Covent Garden, Kemble became joint manager with Harris's son, investing all his money in the venture, but in 1808 Kemble suffered a similar disaster to that which Sheridan was to experience the following year at Drury Lane. In the early morning of September 20, fire broke out in Covent Garden theatre, and by six o'clock 'it was so completely destroyed that you could not have known a building had stood there'. The blaze was sudden and fierce, and in trying to deal with it 23 firemen were killed by the falling roof. Handel's organ was lost, and many of his and Dr. Arne's manuscripts, as well as the entire stock of wine of the Beefsteak Club. Mrs. Siddons, writing later, said to a friend: 'I have lost everything, all my jewels and lace which I have been collecting for thirty years ... all really fine and curious. I had a point veil which had been a toilette of the poor Queen of France, near five yards long ... In short, everything I had in the world of stage ornament is gone, and literally not one vestige is left of all that has cost me so much time and money to collect.'

The sympathy for John Kemble was both sincere and practical. The Prince Regent gave him £1,000, the Duke of Northumberland £10,000. Insurance yielded £50,000 and subscription shares provided the remaining necessary £100,000. On the last day of the year, the foundation stone of Robert Smirke's new theatre was laid, and nine months later it was completed. The design was based on Athene's Temple on the Acropolis. The four fluted columns of the Doric portico were said to be the largest in Europe, apart from those at St. Peter's in Rome. On each side of the portico were bas-reliefs by Flaxman. The auditorium had three tiers of boxes above a circle of private boxes, and the large arch of the proscenium, with its magnificent red velvet curtain, had a span of over 42 feet. The staff included the stage manager, pantomime director, property man and call-boy, scene-painters, carpenters, stage-hands, wardrobe-hands, attendants, lamp-lighters, firemen, porters and the box office staff. It was a brave venture, but it was extremely costly. The play for the opening night was *Macbeth*, and the booking was heavy, but when the public discovered that Kemble, in order to cover his costs, had raised his prices, there was pandemonium.

When the curtain rose, the voices of the players were drowned in 'a continued hissing, groaning, howling, yelling, braying, barking and hooting noise, accompanied by exclamations of "Old prices! No rise! ... No private boxes! ..." The same discordant tumult was repeated on the following evening, and innumerable placards calling for old prices were scattered throughout the theatre'. [5]

On the third evening, Kemble managed to gain a hearing of his turbulent audience and attempted to reason with them. They would have none of it. He closed the theatre for a few days, but when he opened again the demonstrations, with rattles, drums, whistles and cat-calls, were as bad as ever. The public won, for after about two months of similar disturbances Kemble surrendered. The pit was reduced from 4/– to 3/6 and some of the private boxes were removed altogether.

After this bad beginning, however, affairs prospered for Kemble. Henry Bishop became his musical director, adapting many of Scott's novels for the stage as operas. He also revived several of Arne's and Handel's works, as well as *The Beggar's Opera;* and under his direction Covent Garden audiences heard, for the first time, Mozart's *Don Giovanni* and *The Marriage of Figaro*, as well as Rossini's *The Barber of Seville.*

Alternating with these productions, John and Charles Kemble, Mrs. Siddons and Macready were playing Shakespeare, but Mrs. Siddons retired in 1812, Macready in 1816 and John Kemble in 1817, leaving Charles to carry on. Three years later, Harris died, leaving his share of the property to his son, with whom Charles Kemble could not agree. The fortunes of the theatre began to flag, but in 1823 Charles presented a production of *King John*, which was to prove important in theatrical history. The question of historical authenticity in costume and sets was still being debated. John Kemble had made a beginning. Now Charles, with many misgivings, decided to go farther. For *King John* he ordered authentic-looking mail armour and thirteenth century helmets. The audience was delighted, and the way was paved for Charles Kean who, a little later, was to stage his realistic revivals, which aimed at absolute accuracy in every detail of costume and set.

In 1825 a dramatic critic was writing of Covent Garden: 'We are pleased to observe that this house is gradually adopting the French manner of arranging the stage, making a room appear like one by disposing about it articles of furniture. The bedroom scene had an excellent effect last night, though we have much to accomplish before we can hope to rival our neighbours in this respect. We suspect that the improvement already visible may be attributed to Mr. Charles Kemble's visit to Paris.'

Harris's son resigned his part-managership about this time and Charles continued as sole lessee for a while. Bishop's opera *The Maid of Milan*, in which that undying song *Home, sweet Home* occurs, was a great success and then came a production of Weber's *Der Freischutz*. Bishop resigned, after Kemble had refused to increase his salary, and Kemble appointed Weber as his successor, commissioning

[5] *Illustration of the Public Buildings of London*, Vol. I, by Charles Dibdin.

him to write *Oberon*, in which the distinguished Madame Vestris appeared. The opening night of *Oberon*, April 12, 1826, was one of the Garden's great occasions and a triumph for Weber, but he was a sick man and less than a month later he was dead.

Tom Cooke succeeded Weber as musical director, but Kemble now began to run into financial troubles. Gas lighting had been installed in the theatre a few years earlier, but in the 1828-9 season there was a serious explosion in the basement. Kemble had to close the theatre for two weeks, while the old, evil-smelling gas installations were removed and new wax and oil lighting put back for a spell. Kemble struggled on throughout the next year or two, during which time the Duke of Bedford was putting up the market buildings in the Square, but rates and taxes on the theatre were in arrears and then, one day, the bailiffs arrived.

A public appeal saved the theatre. Fanny Kemble, Charles's daughter, revived its fortunes for a while with her brilliant acting, particularly as Juliet, but it was not long before Charles Kemble retired. In 1833 Alfred Bunn, already managing Drury Lane, decided to take over Covent Garden as well. This was the year that Ned Kean, desperately ill, his health broken by drink and dissipation and his powers fast ebbing, made his last appearance. He was playing *Othello*, but he collapsed, and Charles Kean, playing Iago, had to carry his father from the stage.

Alfred Bunn's resources soon came to an end, and during the next few years Osbaldistone, Macready and Charles Matthews, with his wife, Madame Vestris, all tried their hand at the management of Covent Garden theatre. By 1843 it looked like final defeat, for no one could find success and the building was let for a while to the Anti-Corn Law League. Then came good news. At the Italian Opera House in the Haymarket, which, with the accession of Queen Victoria, had come to be known as Her Majesty's, there had been quarrels, difficulties and resignations. The rebels felt that there was room in London for another Italian Opera House, and Persiani, for whose wife Donizetti had written *Lucia di Lammermoor*, found means of raising the money to buy the lease of the Covent Garden theatre and make the necessary alterations to convert it into a full-scale opera house.

By 1847 all was ready. The theatre re-opened as the Royal Italian Opera House, the first manager being Frederick Beale. Jenny Lind was filling the opera house in the Haymarket, but Grisi at Covent Garden was proving herself equally popular. Nevertheless, those early months were a struggle, and by the end of 1848, though receipts were £44,000, expenses had amounted to over £78,000. The management passed to Frederick Gye, and at the end of 1855 he let the theatre to John Anderson, for a ten weeks' season of spectaculars and melodramas. On the last night of Anderson's tenancy, March 4, 1856, he had announced a *Bal Masqué*,

43

Visitors view the remains of the Royal Italian Opera House after its destruction by fire, March 4, 1856

though the dancers were by no means the elegant creatures that the mention of a masked ball usually evokes. They seem to have been a sorry collection of riff-raff, most of whom, by the time the party broke up, were pretty far gone in drink. It was five o'clock in the morning and the National Anthem was being played when the warning cry of *Fire!* was heard. Everyone managed to escape, but the fire engines which raced to Covent Garden from all over London, as the flames lit up the winter sky, could not save the building. The roof collapsed and the theatre was destroyed. Gye alone had lost £30,000. It seemed the end at last for Covent Garden.

However, men like Gye, with a love of the theatre in their blood, are not easily daunted. The shareholders met. Subscriptions were raised. The Duke of Bedford issued a new lease, this time for a somewhat larger site. Plans for a new opera house were soon under way.

This time Edward Barry was the architect. Though the frontage, with its portico and five great Corinthian columns, remained in Bow Street, the theatre, much the same size as La Scala in Milan, was now laid out from east to west, instead of from north to south as formerly. The Flaxman reliefs, which had been saved from the ruins of the old theatre, were replaced on each side of the portico and remain there still. The panel on the left depicts Hecate in her chariot, with Macbeth and Lady Macbeth, and in the niche below stands the figure of Comedy. Below the portico is the panel showing Shakespeare, with Prospero and Caliban, Milton with Samson Agonistes, the Muses, Bacchus, Athene, Aristophanes, Aeschylus and Menander; and on the right, above the statute of Tragedy, is the bas-relief of Pegasus, attended by nymphs.

The portico was originally a carriageway, under which the elegant Victorians and Edwardians were able to step from their carriages under cover. Thence they walked up the crimson carpeted grand stairway to the long, spacious crush bar, with its verandah, now enclosed, opening out over the portico; all white and gold, with deep, rose-coloured curtains and glittering chandeliers.

There was room for an audience of about 1,900 in the new opera house: 497 in the stalls; 136 in the stalls circle, with its 36 boxes; 146 in the grand tier, where there were 33 boxes as well as the royal box and the Duke of Bedford's box; 144 in the balcony stalls of the third tier, which contained 30 boxes; 384 in the amphitheatre, which had eight boxes on either side, and 600 in the gallery. Since then many of the boxes have been cleared away, making additional seating for 200 or more.

The theatre opened on May 15, 1858 with *Les Huguenots*, in which both Grisi and Mario appeared. That opening season was moderately successful, but Gye suffered not only from the rivalry of the Italian Opera in the Haymarket but also from Drury Lane, where E. T. Smith, declaring that Covent Garden was obviously catering now for society, staged a season of Italian Opera 'for the people'. Smith's opera was at popular prices, 4/– for the stalls, 2/6 for the dress circle, 1/– for the pit and second circle and 6d for the galleries.

The search for new talent was keener than ever, and Mapleson at Her Majesty's, who was also backing Smith at Drury Lane, seemed to be finding all the best singers and attaining a higher artistic standard of production. Gye was worried. Grisi's powers were waning. It was clear that she could not hold the stage for much longer. Then, one day in 1861, when Grisi had finally decided to retire, there

45

arrived at Covent Garden a young girl of 18, asking for an audition. She was Adelina Patti. Though she was still only a girl, Gye could not fail to recognize her qualities. Her Covent Garden début as Amina in *La Sonnambula* was a triumph, and that season she also played Violetta and Lucie, as well as singing Zerlina in *Don Giovanni*, for Grisi's last appearance as Donna Anna.

Rivalry between the Haymarket and Covent Garden continued, Mapleson scoring a victory with his first presentation in England of Gounod's *Faust*, which Gye had been given the opportunity to stage but had rejected. In addition to Patti, Gye had Pauline Lucca, Emilia Lagrua, Mario and Fauré. Mapleson had Therese Tietjens, Christine Nilsson, Di Muska, Gassini, Sautey and Ganglini, all of whom had their enthusiastic followers, so that fortune between the two theatres seemed equally divided. Then, on the night of December 7, 1867, Her Majesty's was burnt down and Mapleson was ruined.

After long discussion, Mapleson and Gye joined forces for a year or two, but then Mapleson departed to America and Gye was on his own again. For the next six years he prospered, and Covent Garden became highly fashionable. Attendance at the opera, in the elaborate evening dress affected by the society of Victorian London, with jewels and tiaras, satins and brocades, draped over tightly corseted waists and horse-hair bustles, furs and velvets and long white gloves, became part of the ritual of the social season. Here could be enjoyed the operas of Mozart, Rossini, Gounod, Weber, Donizetti and Verdi, in which Emma Albani, Julian Gayarré and Victor Maurel all rose to stardom. In 1875 Londoners for the first time heard Wagner. This was also the year that the new Carl Rosa Opera Company gave its first season at the Prince's Theatre.

When Gye retired, in 1877, the Opera House was run by his son, Edward. Mapleson was back in England by now and had raised a large sum of money for the building of a new National Opera House near the Embankment, but funds gave out before the theatre was completed. Mapleson had to sell at a heavy loss, for he could raise no more money. The building was pulled down and in its place arose New Scotland Yard. In the meantime, Her Majesty's had been rebuilt and was offering both Italian opera and Wagner.

In London society, Covent Garden Opera House began to decline in popularity. The widowed, ageing Queen never attended and other members of the Royal family showed little taste for opera. Opera stars, though they sang superbly, were often lamentably lacking in acting ability, and prima donnas tended to run to fat. The real opera lovers found the artistic standards of Covent Garden disappointing and discovered more satisfaction in the productions of the Carl Rosa Company, which was now presenting seasons at Drury Lane. Mapleson gave one or two seasons at Covent Garden, but in 1888 Augustus Harris, who had been running Drury Lane for the previous ten years and had been responsible for the Carl Rosa seasons there, now stepped in as manager of the opera house as well.

Harris was a superb showman. The opera house was redecorated, and by careful planning and advance publicity, he managed, on the opening night, to restore to the Garden all its past glories, with the Prince and Princess of Wales attending, together with those members of society who always follow when royalty is present. Harris opened with Verdi's *Aida*, Jean de Reszke singing the part of Radames. His reception proved him to be a worthy successor to Mario, and a few nights later his brother, Edouard, had a similar triumph. During the second week, Harris presented *Lucia di Lammermoor*, and the part of Lucia was played by a new young Australian singer, of whom London had not heard before. She was Nellie Melba, whose success was soon to become as great as that of the illustrious Patti.

Augustus Harris restored the prestige of Covent Garden and once more it took its place as one of the most important opera houses in the world. There had been much controversy concerning the language in which opera should be sung. Hitherto operas had all been sung in Italian, which was considered the only suitable language for great singers, but now there was a change. Operas were sung in the language of their origin, and then there was a movement for some of them to be sung in English translations. With the singing of opera in a variety of languages Covent Garden dropped the title of the Royal Italian Opera House and became the Royal Opera House.

Of the other great names which Harris introduced to Covent Garden during these years, perhaps Tetrazinni is now best remembered. After Harris died in 1896 Drury Lane came under the control of Arthur Collins, but Covent Garden was taken over by a newly formed body, the Grand Opera Syndicate. Maurice Grau was the first managing director, followed in 1902 by André Messager and in 1906 by Forsyth, with Percy Pitt as musical director and coach and Hans Richter as one of its distinguished conductors.

The Covent Garden Syndicate was successful and found money to spare on many improvements to the Opera House, installing new electric lighting in place of gas, and modernizing the stage, which still had an apron and two boxes. These were removed and the additional space given to the orchestra pit. A new flat stage was built, in six sections, of which five were equipped with movable bridges. The roof of the stage was raised and equipped with new lighting and scenery, and the wardrobe was overhauled and replenished.

Between 1897 and 1914, during the grand summer seasons, London heard for the first time *Tosca, Madame Butterfly, Louise, Palleas and Melisande* and *Parsifal*. Caruso, Scotti, Martinelli, John McCormack and Maggie Teyte all made their first Covent Garden appearances. There were also subsidiary seasons, when the Opera house was let to other managements. During one of these *La Bohéme* was introduced and, after 1910, when Thomas Beecham first appeared there, *Elektra*, *Salomé* and *Der Rosenkavalier;* while at Drury Lane Beecham introduced Chaliapine in the Russian operas, *Boris Goudonov, Ivan the Terrible, Prince Igor, May Night, Le Rossignol* and *Le Coq d'Or.*

The Royal Opera House was also presenting, during these pre-war years, Diaghilev's Russian ballet, with Leon Bakst's brilliant decor and colouring, which made so deep an impression, in both Paris and London, that it began a fashion for eastern styles in domestic furnishings and even in women's dress for a while. Then came the First World War. International opera and ballet were over for the next four years, and the gracious and historical Royal Opera House at Covent Garden fell on hard times, being used for a spell as a Government store.

Never was anything so deserted
As this dim theatre . . .

Never was anything so disenchanted
As this silence!
Gleams of soiled gilding on curved balconies
Empty; immense
Dead crimson curtain, tasselled with its old
And staled pretence.[6]

For Covent Garden it was the end of a wonderfully exciting era, when nearly each year brought new and lovely operas, and a succession of glorious singers to do them justice.

During the next twenty years, between the end of the First World War and the outbreak of the Second, opera lovers had plenty of opportunity to hear opera at Covent Garden. During the worst part of the economic depression and the unemployment of the twenties and early thirties, seasons were sometimes short and the display of jewels and gorgeous furs and dresses was less spectacular, but that was all part of the changing social scene. The operas were staged and many brilliant singers were heard there– Melba, Miriam Lycette, Clara Butt, Eva Turner, Olive Gilbert, Florence Austral, Maggie Teyte, Lotte Lehmann, Elizabeth Schumann, Rosa Ponselle, Joan Cross, Mary Jarred, Constance Willis, Oda Slobodskaya, Conchita Supervia, Lily Pons, Kirsten Flagstad, Isobel Baillie and Lisa Perli were amongst the host of international sopranos and contraltos. The tenors, baritones and basses, all of whom were to become part of the story of opera at Covent Garden, included Norman Allin, Martinelli, Percy Heming,

[6]Laurence Binyon.

48

Trefor Evans, Parry Jones, Dennis Noble, Joseph Hislop, Lauritz Melchior, Heddle Nash, Gigli, Laurence Tibbett and Richard Tauber.

Behind the scenes, however, managements were constantly changing and fortunes being lost. It seemed as though no one in England could make opera pay. In 1919 hopes ran high when the Beecham Trust acquired the entire leasehold of Covent Garden, including the market and Drury Lane as well as the opera house. For his opening season, Thomas Beecham conducted for the Grand Opera Syndicate, but the following year he took a sub-lease from the Syndicate for the 1920 season. Artistically it was a success but financially a disaster, and Beecham disappeared from Covent Garden opera for twelve years. The British National Opera Company, which he had formed during the war, leased the theatre for the next few years, alternating with the Carl Rosa Company. Then Courtauld founded the London Opera Syndicate, which leased Covent Garden for the seasons from 1925 to 1927. Another company, the Grand Opera Syndicate, then took a three-year sub-lease from the lease-holders, which was somewhat less disastrous financially than the other ventures, but still did not show a profit.

Beecham, in the meantime, formed his Imperial League of Opera and came forward with a suggestion for joining up with the Covent Garden Opera Syndicate, and it was during these discussions that the first suggestion was heard of a subsidy from the government, but the negotiations dragged on till 1933, by which time the Covent Garden Opera Syndicate's lease had expired.

There was talk of pulling down the Opera House, to make more room for the market. There seemed no room for opera in our cultural life and too many reasons to explain its financial failure at the Garden. These were the days of the cinema boom, for it was only during the 1930s that the first talkies were heard in Britain, promoting a craze which was to bring about the end of so many theatres and music halls. The radio programmes were little more than a decade old and still new enough to keep many people at home. Lilian Baylis's opera and Shakespeare seasons at the Old Vic were gaining steadily in stature, and during the twenties the Old Vic Foundation had bought the site of Sadler's Wells in Islington, where more opera could be heard, at popular prices. There, in the thirties, Ninette de Valois formed her distinguished ballet company, which was before long to gain international fame and implant in so many of the rising generation a deep passion for the ballet. The country was in dire financial difficulties, and although the economic depression lifted somewhat towards the end of the thirties, Britain had still 2,000,000 unemployed. None but the most blindly optimistic could fail to realize that war in Europe was imminent. Times were grim and foreboding, and there was little money to spare for the inevitable losses which seemed to be incurred in the presentation of opera at the Garden.

However, the theatre was saved yet again. Nothing came of the suggestion to extend the market, and yet another new company was formed, the Royal Opera House Company Ltd., which took a new lease of the theatre. Geoffrey Toye was managing director for a while and Lady Cunard was one of the most active members of the Board, which also included Sir Thomas Beecham as artistic director. Extensive improvements were made to the building and a new block of offices, dressing rooms and rehearsal rooms built out at the back of the theatre.

Beecham and Toye disagreed and Toye soon resigned, but Beecham was at Covent Garden till the last season before the war; the summer of 1939. Nearly all the stars of the twenties and thirties were singing at the Garden under Beecham during these years. Among the new names appearing were Elena Danieli, Janet Hamilton-Smith, Marie Burke, William Parsons and Stanley Pope, while for the last season of all, which Beecham financed from his own resources, Gigli made a return. There were many glorious nights of opera during Beecham's reign, and Covent Garden maintained its great traditions nobly, but at the end of it all, when the reckoning came, people were forced to the same melancholy conclusion. Opera did not pay at the Garden.

With the outbreak of war the theatre was closed. Shortly afterwards it was leased by Mecca Cafés and turned into a dance hall for the war years. Nevertheless, it was the long-pent up social force released during the war and the changes it brought into the social order throughout not only Europe but the entire world which ultimately saved the opera house. During the war the Council for the Encouragement of Music and the Arts (CEMA) was founded, under the chairmanship of J. M. Keynes, with money granted, in the first place, by the Pilgrim Trust and later supplemented by the Treasury.

Sadler's Wells escaped the bombing and, under incredible difficulties, Ninette de Valois not only kept the ballet company going but developed and strengthened it till it had acquired its present individuality and distinction. The Old Vic, however, was bombed and put out of action for a while. Financial backing from CEMA enabled it to send four or five companies out on the road to perform Shakespeare and other classical plays, and also opera and ballet supplemented from the Sadler's Wells companies. They reached remote parts of the country which had never before had the opportunity to enjoy such stimulus, and the enthusiasm became real and growing. The Old Vic's London company was established at the New Theatre, and its productions of plays and operas were so successful that the government decided, as peace drew nearer, to continue the grant to CEMA, which now became known as the Arts Council of Great Britain.

This was the first time, in Britain, that the State had ever given patronage to the arts. Within a year or two of the end of the war a National Theatre was

50

established at the newly restored Old Vic and Covent Garden became the National Opera House, for the performance of opera and ballet, the Sadler's Wells company becoming Covent Garden's permanent ballet company.

The task of creating a national opera company was not easy, but under the chairmanship of Lord Keynes the Covent Garden Committee evolved the Covent Garden Opera Trust, which now works in close association with the Arts Council, from which it receives its annual subsidy.

Singers from Sadler's Wells, the Carl Rosa company and the various pre-war Covent Garden companies were assembled under the first musical director of the new régime, Erich Kleiber, and they opened their first season in January, 1947. Musically it was not outstanding, and none of the pre-war elegance of Covent Garden seemed to have survived. Productions were as austere and utilitarian as life itself had become during the late forties, and in the famous crush bar, which once had been the scene of such grace and luxury, men and women in duffle coats and slacks, shapeless pullovers and 'demob' suits jostled each other to grab spam sandwiches and a beer during the interval.

However, the years of austerity passed away at Covent Garden as they did elsewhere, and the quality of both music and production steadily rose. Foreign guest artists and conductors were invited from time to time. New singers appeared and new operas were heard.

Joan Cross, Kathleen Ferrier, Kirsten Flagstad, Elizabeth Schwarzkopf, Adèle Leigh, Victoria de los Angeles, Joan Sutherland, Maria Callas, Joan Hammond, Amy Shuard, Richard Lewis, Peter Pears, Frederick Sharp, Geraint Evans and Tito Gobbi are amongst the great singers who have appeared at the National Opera House. Amongst the new English operas which have been presented are Benjamin Britten's *Peter Grimes*, in 1947, and Arthur Bliss's *The Olympiads* and Britten's *Billy Budd*, both in the 1951-2 season. Britten composed *Gloriana* for the coronation celebrations of Queen Elizabeth II, in 1953, and although it had a mixed reception amongst the music critics the occasion brought back to the old theatre all its traditional glory, for Oliver Messel had provided the most sumptuously beautiful decorations for that opening night. The following season, 1954-5, saw the first nights of William Walton's *Troilus and Cressida* and Michael Tippett's *Midsummer Marriage*.

Covent Garden Opera House is today more firmly established than it ever was, a vigorous, thriving national institution, with permanent national opera and ballet companies, and audiences who attend, not to be seen themselves, in order to establish themselves socially, but because of their deep-felt love of music and the dance.

Chapter 4
Taverns, Coffee Houses and Clubs

WHEN the Earl of Bedford engaged Inigo Jones to lay out the piazzas of Covent Garden and its surrounding streets, there was already a tendency for the rich and aristocratic families of seventeenth century England to move their London homes westwards from the overcrowded city. This was despite government attempts to restrict the building of new houses lest London become too large to govern and control. The spacious mansions which now arose in the new square and in Bedford Street, Russell Street, Tavistock Street, King Street, Henrietta Street and Bow Street therefore filled a real need, and they became for a while a centre of fashion and elegance. Strype wrote that the district was 'well inhabited by a mixture of nobility, gentry and wealthy tradesmen, here seated since the fire of London, scarce admitting of any poor, not very pestered with mean courts and alleys, likewise its open and large piazza and garden so delightful to walk in'.

However, these wealthy households needed shopkeepers, artisans, servants and labourers to maintain them, who very soon were crowding into the district in ever-increasing numbers. For these there was no town-planning, and within a generation their homes were built, huddling close to Inigo Jones's gracious houses, in those 'mean courts and alleys' which Strype had so deplored; a jostle of little buildings, many of which, within a decade, had become poverty-stricken slums, breeding vice and violence

Less than 25 years after the piazzas were built, Richard Broome was writing of 'those venomous weeds that rankly pester the fair garden plot', and early in the eighteenth century Gay wrote:

A view of Covent Garden in the mid-eighteenth century. (Courtesy Covent Garden Market Authority.)

Of Drury's mazy courts and dark abodes,
The harlots' guileful paths who nightly stand,
Where Catherine Street descends into the Strand.

However, in the early years of Covent Garden's glory, nobody seemed to mind what was happening on its very doorstep, and in the houses of the northern Great Piazza and the Little Piazza to the east, the great ones lived in comfort and unconcern. One of the first tenants here was the gallant Sir Edmund Verney, who, during the Civil War, left his beautiful home at Claydon in Buckinghamshire to be King Charles's standard bearer and meet his death at Edgehill. Sir Edmund had

53

rented two houses in the Little Piazza from the Earl of Bedford, where later was to stand the Bedford Coffee House.

Among a score of Sir Edmund's neighbours, all of them marquises and earls, baronets and knights, was Sir Kenelm Digby, son of Sir Everard who at the beginning of the century had been hanged, along with Guy Fawkes, for his part in the Gunpowder Plot. Sir Kenelm's house, the last on the north side of King Street, adjoining the Great Piazza, had already had several distinguished tenants, including Tom Killigrew. It was the loveliest in the square and, though sadly altered, is still standing.

During the seventeenth century Sir Peter Lely and Sir Godfrey Kneller both had houses in the piazzas, and Kneller's house, in the north-east corner, where the Floral Hall of the market now stands, passed in time to Sir James Thornhill, the father-in-law of Hogarth, who, as a youth, had come to Thornhill's house for art classes. Also living in the square at the same time as Hogarth was the unfortunate Richard Wilson who, though he is known today as the father of British landscape painting, could not make a living by his painting during his lifetime, and at last, in poverty and despair, had to move to an attic off the Tottenham Court road. There he subsisted mainly on bread and porter[1], until some sympathetic relatives rescued him and took him down to their home in Wales for his remaining years.

Coffee became a fashionable drink in England during the seventeenth century, after the merchant ships of the East India Company had brought the first consignments to London. To the consternation of the vintners, coffee houses were soon established, the first appearing in Cornhill in 1652. Many more were soon opened, and by the beginning of the eighteenth century there were more than 500 of them, including several famous ones in Covent Garden. By this time, the upper crust of the aristocracy had begun to move away from Covent Garden to the mansions of Mayfair, which were being built farther west, in Hanover Square, Cavendish Square and Grosvenor Square. In their place came members of the upper classes, men of letters and politics, the theatre and the arts. The coffee houses which came into existence in Covent Garden were, particularly in the early days of the fashion, the meeting places of these intellectuals. As they drank they gambled and talked endlessly, often brilliantly.

In its heyday, Will's was the most famous. It stood at the northern corner of Russell Street and Bow Street and had formerly been a tavern. The ground floor was a haberdasher's shop, but on the first floor Will Urwin opened his coffee shop. Dryden was his most distinguished client, one of the few men of letters who was accepted, during his lifetime, as the greatest writer of his day, and it was Dryden who made Will Urwin's fortune. Will's customers were seated, for the

[1]Dark-brown beer brewed from charred or browned malt.

most part, in groups at tables, but Dryden had the place of honour, by the fire in winter, and in a corner of the balcony overlooking the street in summer.

Dryden was born in 1631. While still in his twenties, after graduating from Cambridge, where he was a friend of Pepys, he arrived in Covent Garden to write for Drury Lane theatre and, in due time, to succeed Davenant as Poet Laureate. He was a friend not only of most of the aristocracy but of King Charles himself, and after he had married Lady Elizabeth Howard he made his home in Long Acre. It was his habit to work all the morning, dine with his family about three o'clock in the afternoon, and spend the rest of the day at Will's, drinking coffee and talking, for the amusement of himself and his friends and also for the benefit of the rest of Will's customers. So distinguished did the company of listeners become, when Dryden held court, that although Will's did not have the rules and subscription of the clubs which were soon to come into existence, it was, in essence, one of the first literary clubs of London, and few would have presumed to visit it without a proper introduction.

Pope, who was not born till 1688, had so deep an admiration for the great Dryden that he persuaded his friends to take him to Will's, to gaze upon the great man. Dryden died in 1700, so Pope cannot have been more than 12 at the time, but he never forgot that visit.

By the time he was 17, Pope, already a poet of distinction and with his own following, was visiting Will's on his own account, but the coffee house was never the same after Dryden's death. Jonathan Swift, a distant relative of Dryden, though 30 years younger, wrote sourly of the company he found there in later years. The worst conversation he ever heard in his life, he said, 'was at Will's Coffee-house, where the wits (as they were called) used formerly to assemble; that is to say, five or six men, who had writ plays or at least prologues, or had a share in a miscellany, came thither, and entertained one another with their trifling composures, in so important an air as if they had been the noblest efforts of human nature, or that the fate of kingdoms depended on them.'

It was only for about ten years after Dryden's death that Will's maintained its old prestige. Then Button's coffee house, on the opposite side of Russell Street, had its day. Addison and Steele, both born in 1678, were coming into their own and Button's, which opened in 1712, was their meeting place. Pope joined them there for a while but could not stand the pace. 'Addison usually studied all the morning,' said Pope, 'then met his party at Button's, dined there, and stayed five or six hours; and sometimes far into the night. I was of the company for about a year, but found it too much for me; it hurt my health, and so I quitted it.'

The gentle, kindly Steele had already made literary history with his publication, in 1709, of the *Tatler*, the first important English periodical, in the production

55

No. 43 *King Street, at the time when it was tenanted by Lord Archer.*
(Courtesy Covent Garden Market Authority.)

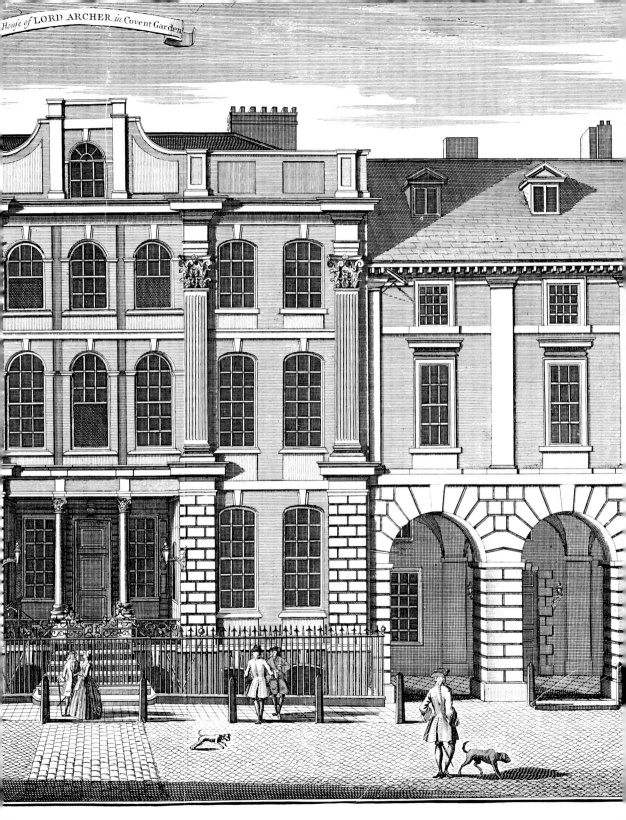

House of LORD ARCHER in Covent Garden

of which Addison had given him valuable help. The *Tatler* appeared three times a week until 1711, and then Addison and Steele together produced its successor, the *Spectator*, which was a daily, to be followed two years later by the short-lived *Guardian*, for which they invited contributions to be sent to Button's.

They placed at the entrance of the coffee house a lion's head with a large open mouth, into which aspiring authors placed their contributions. These fell into the box held in the lion's paw, propped below its chin. 'Whatever the Lion swallows, I shall digest for the use of the public', declared Addison.

Swift frequented Button's, and also Defoe and Colley Cibber. These early years of the eighteenth century were a wonderful time for English literature and letter-writing, and it was Covent Garden which nurtured the inspiration. In 1717, Lady Mary Wortley Montagu began writing her delightful letters from Constantinople and the Near East, in one of which she advocated the Turkish habit of innoculation against smallpox. In London, this disease was becoming as great a scourge as the plague had been in the previous century. When she and her husband returned to England, the following year, they lived for a while at Twickenham, where Pope had by now established himself and created his beautiful garden. Pope was greatly attracted to Lady Mary and wrote her long and amorous letters, but when she ignored them, or, even worse, made fun of them, he turned on her all the waspish venom and jealousy which he had shown towards Addison and Steele at Button's. The Montagus left Twickenham, and by 1730 Lady Mary had become one of the residents of the piazzas of Covent Garden.

Button's continued to prosper till Addison died in 1719 and Steele retired to Wales. Then poor Daniel Button fell on hard times. His business dwindled and he was soon receiving parish relief from St. Paul's. He died in 1731, was buried at St. Paul's and Button's coffee house was no more.

While Button's was at the height of its success, there was another coffee house, only a few doors away, with an equally distinguished clientèle. This was Tom's, at Number 14, Russell Street, where, during the reign of Queen Anne, 'there was playing at piquet, and the best of conversation till midnight'. It was the resort of members of the Court and 'its balcony in the daytime was often crowded with members of the Upper House of Parliament, who came thither to drink tea and coffee and to be amused'.

Tom's continued to be popular with succeeding generations of Covent Garden people throughout the eighteenth century. Early in the 1760s a club was established there, which included amongst its members Garrick, Foote, Murphy' Goldsmith, Dr. Johnson, the Duke of Montague, Lord Rodney, Lord Clive and the Duke of Northumberland. It continued as a coffee house for many years after these great names had passed into history and was not finally closed until 1814.

When Button's closed, many of its old customers moved to the Bedford coffee house, which had been converted from Sir Edmund Verney's old house in the Little Piazza. It was next door to the piazza entrance to John Rich's new Covent Garden theatre and became the resort of the playwrights and actors. Here Addison's lion's head from Button's was installed for a while, till it passed into other hands and eventually came into the possession of the Bedford family.

A writer in *The Connoisseur*, in 1754, said of the Bedford: 'This coffee house is crowded every night with men of parts. Almost everyone you meet is a polite scholar and wit; jokes and bon-mots are echoed from box to box; every branch of literature is critically examined, and the merit of every production of the press, or performance at the theatres, weighed and determined. This school . . . has bred up many authors to the amazing entertainment and instruction of their readers.'

During the 1750s, Foote was the most brilliant of the talkers there. Regular customers always tried to sit as close as possible to his table or, better still, to be invited to join his party at supper, for he was carelessly lavish in his hospitality. Here also came his rival, Garrick, as well as Quin, Macklin and Sheridan, but Macklin retired from the stage for a while and set up a coffee house of his own, the Piazza, in the north-east corner of the square, which once had been Sir Godfrey Kneller's house.

Macklin opened in 1754, announcing a public ordinary to be served each day at four o'clock, for 3/–, which included port, claret or any other liquor. Poor Macklin had grandiose ideas which did not work. As the clock struck four each day, a bell rang for five minutes and then the order was given to the kitchen to serve the meal. Ten minutes later it was on the table and the doors were closed to any other visitors. Macklin himself, in full dress suit, always carried in the first dish, and when he had set it before his guests he retired to the sideboard, to keep a watchful eye on his waiters, who had been instructed to make no sound as they worked, so that the guests' enjoyment should not in any way be impaired. Macklin strove to feed his clients' souls and minds, as well as their bodies, for he announced a series of after-dinner debates on the arts, sciences, literature, criticism, philosophy, history, politics and morality. He stated that 'Mr. Macklin intends to lecture upon the comedy of the ancients, the use of their masks and flutes, their mimes and pantomimes, and the use and abuse of the stage. He will likewise lecture on the rise and progress of modern theatres, making a comparison between them and those of Greece and Rome, and between each other; he also proposes to lecture upon each of Shakespeare's plays.'

It was not to be, for no one wanted to hear him. Nine months later Macklin was bankrupt and returned to the stage, but the Piazza coffee house, passing into other hands, prospered and became a favourite resort of Sheridan and later of Kemble.

Next door to the Piazza was the Shakespeare, said to be the first tavern ever to be opened in Covent Garden, which was famous for its magnificent cooking and, in particular, its turtle soup. It was also the scene of the last act of one of Covent Garden's tragedies. The story began some 30 years earlier, when Lord Sandwich, passing through Covent Garden one day, had noticed behind the counter of a milliner's shop in Tavistock Street a beautiful young girl named Reay. He fell madly in love with her, and had her educated. She became his mistress. He even took her to his home in Huntingdonshire, where he introduced her to his family, much to the distress of Lady Sandwich. Here she met the gay and handsome Captain Hackman, who loved her dearly and proposed marriage, but Miss Reay would have none of him. She remained faithful to Lord Sandwich and returned with him to London, to the establishment he had provided for her.

Hackman resigned his commission and took Holy Orders, but throughout the passing years his passion for Miss Reay persisted. He came to London and tried to resume his friendship with her, but once more she repulsed him. In desperation, like many another rejected lover, he kept a watch on her movements. On April 7, 1779, Miss Reay drove to Covent Garden theatre to see *Love in a Village*. Hackman, from a coffee house in Cockspur Street, saw the carriage pass and followed. He watched her enter the theatre, and throughout the performance he hung about in the vestibule or in the Bedford coffee house next door. At the end of the evening, as she was leaving the theatre and just about to step into her carriage, Hackman rushed out of the Bedford, shot her and turned the pistol on himself. Miss Reay fell dead but Hackman's own wound was only slight. They were both carried into the Shakespeare, and when Hackman realized what he had done he frenziedly tried to kill himself again, but was restrained. His wounds were dressed. At five o'clock in the morning Sir John Fielding arrived from Bow Street and committed him to the Bridewell at Tothill Fields. He was tried for murder and condemned to death. On his last journey to Tyburn, James Boswell, who had a great fancy for hangings, accompanied him in the mourning coach.

Boswell was full of admiration for the calm fortitude with which Hackman met his death, and quoted the case as a solemn warning of the dreadful effects that the passion of love may produce, the affair being all the more remarkable since poor Miss Reay, at the time of her murder, was at least 45 and had borne the earl nine children, of whom six were still living.

Admiral Russell, Earl of Orford, who followed the romantic and eccentric Sir Kenelm Digby at 43 King Street, the gracious Inigo Jones house adjoining the Great Piazza, was one of its most distinguished tenants. He had achieved fame by

60

his victory over the French at La Hogue, which had put an end to the hopes of the Jacobites in France and ensured the safety of the throne for William III. He was a staunch Whig, and meetings of influential members of the party were held at his house in Covent Garden, from which were to develop the first Cabinet Councils.

Admiral Russell died in 1727. The next two tenants of the house were Lord Archer and James West, the President of the Royal Society, who died in 1772. Then the house was turned into a hotel, said to be the first of its kind in London. The first proprietor was a hairdresser from Southampton Street, David Low, who could not make it pay, but subsequent owners made it a place of high fashion, known as the Star, because of its illustrious visitors. Then, early in the nineteenth century, W. C. Evans, a comedian from Covent Garden theatre, took over and it became the highly successful Evans' Hotel and Supper Rooms. When Evans retired, in 1844, Paddy Green succeeded, and in 1856 built a music hall out at the back of the building, over part of Sir Kenelm Digby's garden. Here, in the years between, a small cottage had been built in which Charles Kemble and his wife had lived for a while and where the gifted Fanny had been born.

Evans' music hall seems to have been conducted with extraordinary decorum, for an account of a visit there in 1867 says: 'Ladies are not admitted, except on giving their names and addresses, and then only enjoy the privilege of watching the proceedings from behind a screen. The whole of the performances are sustained by the male sex, and an efficient choir of men and boys sing glees, ballads and madrigals and selections from operas, the accompaniments being supplied on the piano and harmonium . . . On the occasion of our last visit to "Evans's" we heard standard music, English, German and Italian, performed with admirable spirit, precision and delicacy. The performances commence at eight o'clock; and we recommend Evans's to the notice of steady young men who admire a high class of music, see no harm in a good supper, but avoid theatres and the ordinary run of music-halls . . .'

It was at a room in Evans' that the Savage Club was formed, in 1857, and held its first meetings before moving to the Adelphi. Amongst the first Savages, who could think of no better or more pretentious name to describe themselves, were George Augustus Sala, George Grossmith, Tom Robertson and W. S. Gilbert. When the Adelphi was pulled down the club moved to Carlton House Terrace, but now, after more than a century, it has moved back to Covent Garden, to a house in King Street only a few doors from the place where it was born.

Evans' music hall and the adjoining hotel lasted until 1880. Then they were taken over for a while by the Falstaff Club and later by the New Club, but in

61

The music hall in Evans' Hotel at 43 King Street in the mid-nineteenth century. (Courtesy Covent Garden Market Authority.)

1891 they became the headquarters of the National Sporting Club, which remained there till 1933, when the historic old house was bought by one of the market firms, George Monro. The doorway was removed and the ground floor drastically altered, to make it suitable for its present use as a sales room, but the frontage still stands, after more than 300 years.

Many of the old London coffee houses had become hotels by the nineteenth century, and in Covent Garden the Piazza coffee house became the Tavistock Hotel, which was an institution for many years, till it was pulled down to make

GROUND FLOOR PLAN

FIRST FLOOR PLAN

The New Hummums. (Courtesy Covent Garden Market Authority.)

room for the Floral Hall of the market. There were several other hotels in Covent Garden, of which the best known were the Hummums, the Old and the New. The Old Hummums was originally a Turkish bath establishment, on the south-west corner of Russell Street, facing the market and part of the Little Piazza. It was built in the early days of Covent Garden and for a while was very popular amongst the residents, but it soon fell on evil times. It became dirty and neglected and haunted by the prostitutes of Drury Lane and thereabouts. In 1701 a new manage-ment took over, announcing: 'The Hummums in Covent Garden having for several years been neglected and abused by those persons that had the care and manage-ment of them, whereby several persons of quality have been disgusted, and have left off coming thither to sweat and bathe as formerly: This is to give notice, that the said Hummums are now in possession of others who have refitted the same and rectified all those neglects and abuses that were formerly done there, where persons may sweat and bathe in the cleanliest, and be cupped after the newest, manner. There is likewise provided good lodging for any persons who shall desire to lodge there all night, where who pleases may see the same. The price as was always, for sweating and bathing, is 5/6, for two in one room, 8/–: but who lodges there all night 10/–.'

The Old Hummums became a hotel but in 1865 it was pulled down and the site used for market buildings. The New Hummums was built next door. For many a year to come it was a favourite place for young men to finish off a night on the Town and sober down, but that, too, has now gone, before the ever-increasing demands of the market for more space.

Many of the groups of politicians, artists, writers and actors who frequented the coffee houses formed themselves into clubs, but other coffee houses de-generated into ordinary taverns. There were taverns which were as well run as the coffee houses had been, but others were notorious for the evil of their frequenters. So it came about that in Covent Garden there were coffee houses as disreputable as the worst of the taverns, and taverns where men of letters and distinction met regularly and peaceably.

Tom King's coffee house, in front of St. Paul's Church, was one of the worst, and little more than a brothel. Tom King was well born, but had run away from Eton and married the notorious Moll King. After Tom's death she ran the coffee house on her own. Here the rakes of the town used to meet in the early hours of the morning. Moll would provide them with prostitutes, making the place so disreputable that, in 1739, she was finally arrested, charged with keeping a disorderly house and committed to the King's Bench prison. The Finish, on the south side of the square, kept by Mrs. Butler, was no better, and here footpads and highwaymen used to mix with the wealthy young bloods. Mother Douglas's,

Tom King's Coffee House early in the morning, according to Hogarth.

on the north side, was as bad, and Mother Douglas was believed to be the original of Mrs. Cole in Cleland's *Fanny Hill*. The Rose in Russell Street had a bad name 'as the resort of the worst characters of the town, both male and female, who made it the headquarters of midnight orgies and drunken broils, where murderous assaults were frequently occurring among the bullies of the time', and this was the place that Hogarth depicted in his third scene of *The Rake's Progress*. Mrs. Gould's and Hell-Fire Stanhope's hostelries were equally notorious for gambling, wenching and the drinking of cheap gin, which by the 1740s was causing the death of one in eight Londoners, prompting one enterprising tavern proprietor, according to Tobias Smollett, to put up a notice which read: 'Here you may get drunk for a penny, dead drunk for twopence, and get straw for nothing.'

A quick run through the main streets of Covent Garden shows the extraordinary way in which its distinguished literary, artistic and theatrical history flourished alongside the profligacy, gambling and debauchery.

In St. Martin's Lane lived Sir John Suckling and Sir Kenelm Digby, for a while, and later it was the home of Sir Joshua Reynolds, before he moved to Leicester Square. At the Sutherland Arms, in a small court off the Lane, the Eccentric Club, whose members included Fox, Sheridan, Melbourne and Brougham, had their meetings. In Chandos Street, at the corner of Bedford Street, was the Three Tuns, where Sally Salisbury, 'the most notorious woman that ever infested the Hundreds of Old Drury or Covent Garden either', in 1723 stabbed the Honourable John Finch, and died in Newgate prison. This tavern had been a resort of Pepys, as was also the Rose in Russell Street and the Fleece in York Street, 'a tavern most unfortunate for homicides'. Also in Chandos Street was the Hole-In-The-Wall, where the Marquis of Granby now stands. In the seventeenth century the Hole-In-The-Wall was kept by Mother Maberley, a cast-off mistress of the Duke of Buckingham, and here, in 1669, Claude Duval, the Gentleman Highwayman, was arrested and brought to trial.

At Number 3 Chandos Street was the blacking factory where, early in the nineteenth century, that unhappy small boy, Charles Dickens, was first sent to work, when he was 12 years old and his father was lodged in the Marshalsea prison for debt. Penniless and forlorn, he nevertheless developed his love of Covent Garden during these sad months. 'When I had no money I took a turn in Covent Garden and stared at the pineapples,' he said.

Bedfordbury, that dismal little street leading from Chandos Street into New Street (now New Row), was respectable enough when it was first built during the reign of Charles I, but it declined lamentably and was probably the place which Dickens described in *Bleak House*, where Tom-All-Alone used sometimes to retreat: 'It is a black, dilapidated street, avoided by all decent people; where the

66

crazy houses were seized upon when their decay was far advanced, by some bold vagrants, who, after establishing their own possession, took to letting them out in lodgings. Now these tumbling tenements contain, by night, a swarm of misery.'

New Row, the westerly extension of King Street, is where Flaxman was born, at his father's plaster shop, and it was from here that he sent his first model of a man's head to the Royal Academy. At the Pineapple Samuel Johnson, when he first came to London, used to dine for 8d., giving 6d. for a cut of meat, 1d. for bread and 1d. for the waiter.

Close by, in Rose Street, Samuel Butler, the author of *Hudibras*, which Samuel Pepys tried so valiantly to understand and enjoy, lived and died: and it was here that Dryden was brutally cudgelled, on his way home to Long Acre.

Bedford Street, which was to become the home of so many booksellers and publishers, was, from the beginning, a far wider, more handsome and prosperous thoroughfare. One of its earliest residents was Thomas Sheridan, father of Richard, and here Dr. Johnson was a visitor. James Quin lived in Bedford Street and Edward Kynaston retired here, to live with his son, who was a mercer. The most famous tavern in the street was the Constitution, a favourite haunt of Richard Wilson and his friend, Dr. Arne; and at Wildman's coffee house the followers of John Wilkes used to meet.

King Street has many memories. James Quin was born here in 1793 and Dr. Arne in 1710, at the house of his father, who was an upholsterer. Samuel Taylor Coleridge lived here for three years, while writing for the *Morning Post*, and also Charles Dibdin, whose most famous song was *Tom Bowling*. From 1743 till 1745 it was the home of David Garrick and many years later, in 1830, the Garrick Club held its first meetings at Number 35, one of its earliest members being William Thackeray. The club remained here till it moved to its present home in Garrick Street in 1864.

King Street was the street of hotels and coffee houses, book sellers, publishers and auctioneers, and amongst the auctioneers, Debenham Storr and Johnson Dymond Ltd. still remains, at Number 26, on the corner running into Garrick Street.

It was in King Street that mahogany was first used by cabinet makers. In the middle of the eighteenth century, the story goes that 'Dr. Gibbons an eminent physician of the time, was building a house in King Street, when his brother, a West Indian captain, brought over some mahogany as ballast, and thinking the wood might be of service to his brother, the doctor, he sent him a quantity of it; but the carpenters finding it too hard to work, it was laid aside. Soon after this, Mrs. Gibbons wanting a candle-box, the doctor called on his cabinet maker in Long Acre, and asked him to make one of some wood that lay in his garden. He complained, however, that it was too hard for his tools, and the doctor said he must get stronger tools. The box was made and approved, so that the doctor had a bureau made of the same wood; the fine colour and polish were so pleasing that he invited his friends to come and see the bureau; and among them was the Duchess of Buckingham, through whose patronage of it the wood came into general use.'[2]

After 1753 mahogany was imported in large quantities from the West Indies and used extensively by the great furniture makers of the time, the Adam brothers, Chippendale, Sheraton and Hepplewhite. The Chippendale workshops were established at 62 St. Martin's Lane in 1753, where they remained till 1813. Many of the houses of Covent Garden, particularly in King Street, had mahogany front doors, and in Goodwin's Court, that delightful little row of bow-fronted houses leading eastwards from St. Martin's Lane, they remain to this day. A great many of the interior doors of the old Covent Garden houses are still of mahogany, including many in the charming little house of Abelard-Schuman, the publishers, leading off its steep and narrow and crazily winding staircase.

During the first half of the seventeenth century one of the most distinguished residents of Henrietta Street was the unfortunate Lord Strafford, and a few years later, Pepys was visiting Samuel Cooper, the miniature painter, here. At Rawthmell's coffee house the Society of Arts was established, in 1754, at the time when Kitty Clive was living in the street. Hannah More, a member of the Blue Stocking Club and friend of Garrick and Sheridan, lived in Henrietta Street in her younger days. Later still, at the turn of the century, Jane Austen sometimes stayed at Number 10, above the bank of which her brother was a partner, next door to where Fannie Kelley was living. She was the beautiful actress from Covent Garden whom Charles Lamb loved so dearly and begged in vain to marry him.

At the Castle Tavern in Henrietta Street Sheridan fought a duel with Captain Matthews, who had spoken disparagingly of Miss Linley, Sheridan's future wife, and at Number 23 was Offley's, famous for its Burton ale and the size and succulence of its mutton chops. Offley had once been employed at Bellamy's Chop and Coffee House, adjoining the old House of Commons, where members used to eat and drink and fill in time during dull debates, making it their club. Offley's became Bellamy's greatest rival, the older establishment being immortalized in Pitt's last words: 'I think I could eat one of Bellamy's chops.' After Charles Dickens began to prosper, Offley's was one of his favourite haunts, but after Offley retired the place was closed and became the first home of Macmillan, the publisher.

Maiden Lane today is a sad, dull little street, but it was once the home of

2Quoted in *Annals of Covent Garden* by E. Beresford Chancellor, Hutchinson, 1930.

Andrew Marvell, and fifty years later, when Voltaire was lodging there, at the sign of the White Peruke, a French wig-maker's, he was visited by Pope, Swift and Congreve. In 1775, the year in which Charles Lamb and Jane Austen were born, there was also born, at Number 26, the greatest English artist of his day, Turner.

No. 26 Maiden Lane, birthplace of William Turner. (Courtesy Covent Garden Market Authority.)

In 1820 a poor Jewish boy, Moses Moses, was born in London. He, too, came to live in Maiden Lane, as a dealer in secondhand clothes. Moses was no ordinary, seedy, rag-and-bone merchant. He was a liberal Jew, highly intelligent, a fair dealer and possessed of that keen eye for quality which is a characteristic of so many Jews. He was hard-working and, in a modest way, successful, and by the time his sons were old enough to help him in the business, he had already earned a name for giving good value. In 1881 the family moved its business to a shop on the corner of Bedford Street and King Street, and when old Moses died, in 1894, two of his boys, Alfred and George, continued the business in secondhand clothes, changing their name to Moss.

They bought the clothes and uniforms of old soldiers and men of rank whose estates and effects came to be auctioned at Debenham Storr, across the road, and other nearby auction rooms. They bought Savile Row tailors' misfits, which rich and exacting clients had rejected. Then, one day, in 1897, a friend of Alfred's, Charles Pond, who had failed on the stock exchange and was down on his luck, found that he could get engagements as an entertainer. The only trouble was that he had pawned his dress suit. Alfred Moss, always generous, offered to lend him one from the business. Charles Pond prospered, and when he was well able to afford a dress suit of his own again, he suggested to Alfred that he would prefer to hire one from him, for half a guinea a night, the charge to include the pressing and cleaning of the suit and replacement when necessary. Alfred agreed, and from this simple beginning the largest hire service in the world developed.

In 1899 Alfred and George rebuilt their old corner shop, and for the first time the words Moss Bros. appeared over the door. Moss Bros. became part of the friendly, generous Covent Garden scene and its fame was destined to become world-wide. The business has remained in the family, and today there are about 1,000 employees, in 16 branches scattered throughout the country.

The firm also began a man's ready-to-wear tailoring business of its own. When the 1914 war broke out, they found that they had a sufficient stock of service uniforms stored away to open a military department. They bought up cloth, engaged more staff and within a few weeks were guaranteeing to provide a uniform in 36 hours. Moreover, they were able to equip an officer with nearly all his needs, from a Sam Browne belt to tropical camping gear.

After the war, the ready-to-wear tailoring department continued to flourish, but the hire service expanded with remarkable speed. Men were at first diffident at being seen at Moss Bros., but as more and more people availed themselves of the firm's service, providing top hats and morning coats for weddings and for Ascot, in an astonishing range of sizes, and expensive Court dress for the rare occasions on which a man might need it, the prejudices were soon overcome. Moss Bros. took over the business of Thomas Palmer, the saddler of Upper St. Martin's Lane, opened a saddlery department and were soon stocking all the equipment for riding and hunting as well.

In 1939 they were better prepared with uniforms for the new rush of demand, and during the austere years of clothes rationing they proved invaluable.

After the war they opened a women's department and now run a flourishing business in women's ready-to-wear clothes, as well as in the hire of wedding dresses, bridesmaids' dresses and evening frocks. An American commentator at the

Coronation of Queen Elizabeth estimated that at least 1,000 of the Abbey congregation had been dressed in King Street, and declared that 'without Moss Bros. Queen Elizabeth's Coronation could scarcely have taken place'.

A year or two later, *The Economist* was remarking that 'it would be a fair guess to say that three-quarters of the men who wore morning dress at Ascot this week were not wearing their own clothes . . . at the Eton and Harrow match, even, it must be said, a large proportion of old Etonians will have packed up their clothes in a neat parcel for return to a West End hiring firm on Monday morning . . . Making all allowances for British snobbery and our latent love of pageantry, it is difficult to believe in the permanence of a social convention that requires people to wear clothes that hardly anyone nowadays even pretends to own'. Maybe. Maybe not. Moss Bros. grew by accident. It saw a demand and filled it. And the odd thing is that, despite the aggressive democracy and egalitarianism of the times, the demand still grows. Perhaps there is more to this delight in dressing up than meets the eye.

There were two famous taverns in Maiden Lane, the Cider Cellars and the Bedford Head, both opened in 1730. Amongst the regular customers of the Cider Cellars were Louis Napoleon, Benjamin Disraeli and Thackeray. It retained its good name till the middle of the nineteenth century, when it was demolished to make room for the enlarged Adelphi theatre; though on part of the site the Adelphi Club was established. The stage door of the Adelphi is at the weatern end of Maiden Lane, and it was here, in 1897, that William Terriss, father of Ellaline Terriss, was murdered by a madman as he was leaving the theatre after a performance of *Black-eyed Susan*.

At the Bedford Head, Voltaire was a frequent visitor, and Hogarth, Churchill, Fielding and Goldsmith established their Shilling Rubber Club here. In its heyday, it was the meeting place of most of the great writers and artists of the time, including Walpole and Pope. The original building, which was demolished in 1870, once extended round the corner into Southampton Street.

At Number 35, on the north side of the street, Rules still flourishes. The restaurant and oyster bar was established in 1798, in a building which is now 250 or more years old, where once there was a coffee shop. Rules claims to have been longer in business than any other restaurant in London. It is in the tradition of Romano's and Gatti's, small, intimate and cosy, still with its crimson velvet banquettes.

Little is known of Mr. Rule or the two sons who succeeded him in the business, but from its first years the restaurant became a favourite meeting place of men of letters and the theatre. Thackeray often dined here, as well as Dickens, Douglas Jerrold and a host of distinguished nineteenth-century journalists, and

Leopold Wagner described it, with more enthusiasm than accuracy, as 'the earliest rendezvous for superior intelligences of which we possess any record'.

William Bayliss, the proprietor who succeeded the Rules, made the restaurant into a minor theatrical museum, for the walls are covered with prints, playbills and portraits. On the ground floor, in addition to the Dighton and Rowlandson prints and the Spy cartoons, are portraits of Madame Vestris and Charles Matthews and a number of other famous players. Amongst the playbills is one announcing Lord Lytton's *Not so Bad as We Seem*, which was performed at the Hanover Square Rooms in the summer of 1851 by a distinguished caste of amateurs, which included Dickens, Douglas Jerrold, Mark Lemon, Wilkie Collins and Sir John Tenniel. Another, from Drury Lane, dated 1776, announces Garrick as Richard III, with Mrs. Siddons appearing for the first time as Lady Anne.

On the first floor, with its Hogarth prints of *Marriage à la Mode*, is the curtained alcove where Edward VII, as Prince of Wales, used to dine with Lily Langtry. It was approached by a specially-made doorway at the head of the narrow, dark stairway, so that the Prince could enter without pasing into the main restaurant. On the second floor is the small, low-ceilinged, panelled banqueting room, with its prints of Hogarth's *The Rake's Progress* and its own treasured silver and glass, reserved for occasions of ceremony and celebration.

A few years ago, the ground floor of the restaurant was extended into the next building, which was of about the same age, but none of the old atmosphere has been lost and today Rules is as popular amongst theatre people and others as it ever was.

It was at the laboratories of a firm of chemists and druggists on the south side of Maiden Lane that, during the latter part of the seventeenth century, Robert Boyle demonstrated his 'Boyle's Law', and on this site now stands the Roman Catholic Chapel of Corpus Christi, which was opened by Cardinal Manning in 1874.

Southampton Street was the home of David Garrick and his wife for more than 20 years, and of Congreve, Mrs. Oldfield, Dick Estcourt and Thomas Linley, Sheridan's father-in-law; while in 1836 W. S. Gilbert was born there.

Tavistock Street during the eighteenth century was renowned principally for its fashionable mercers' and milliners' shops, but it also had a famous tavern, the Salutation, where the Prince Regent used to meet Lord Surrey and Sheridan. Today the shops are all part of the market.

Continuing eastwards, Dr. Johnson lodged in Exeter Street when he first came to London; and in Charles Street, which has now disappeared into Wellington Street, Colley Cibber once lived at Number 3 with Barton Booth next door.

Catherine Street did not stay respectable for long. Even by eighteenth century standards it was considered a bad spot, the resort of thieves and prostitutes and even murderers. The Fleece had been closed down by the end of the seventeenth century, but the Rose, next door to Drury Lane theatre, where Hogarth and Gay found much of their inspiration, remained till 1775. Then, when Robert Adam enlarged the theatre for Garrick, the wicked old place was pulled down.

In York Street, connecting Catherine Street with Tavistock Street, De Quincey wrote his *Confessions of an Opium Eater*, and it was here that Charles Lamb visited him, from his lodgings in nearby Russell Street, where he was writing his *Essays of Elia*.

At the corner of Broad Street and Bow Street stood the Wrekin tavern, where Douglas Jerrold's Mulberry Club met to give papers on Shakespeare. The Mulberries became the Shakespeare Club, which was to include in its members Charles Dickens and William Godwin, then living in Tavistock Street, who was later to marry Mary Wollstonecraft and become the father-in-law of Shelley, but in 1871 the Wrekin was pulled down.

One other great literary event of Covent Garden was in 1841 when, at the Crown Tavern in Crown Court, *Punch* was born and Mark Lemon became its first editor.

Most of the literary and political clubs which came to life in Covent Garden have long since died. One of the most illustrious was the Beefsteak Club, founded by John Rich and his scene painter, Lambert, in 1735, shortly after they had moved from Lincoln's Inn Fields to the new theatre in Covent Garden. The club, limited to 25 members, which included, in its time, the Prince Regent, Sheridan, Garrick, Lord Sandwich, John Wilkes, Hogarth, John Thornhill and the Dukes of Argyll and Leinster, met regularly at the theatre each week, to eat, with great ceremony, the choicest beefsteaks. After the first fire at Covent Garden, they moved to the Bedford coffee house next door, then to the Shakespeare's Head in Russell Street and finally to the Lyceum, which had been opened as a hall for entertainments of various kinds in 1771 and rebuilt and licensed as a theatre in 1834. Here the Beefsteaks remained till the club was brought to an end in 1859.

However, the Garrick and the Savage survived and today are as flourishing as ever.

The social reforms of the nineteenth and twentieth centuries wrought so many changes in Covent Garden that the sites of many of the old streets and taverns are now difficult to trace. The Lamb and Flag in Rose Street and the White Swan in New Row are two of the oldest survivals, though neither seems to have had any particular literary or theatrical associations. With the cutting of Kingsway through to the Strand and the building of Aldwych, and with the creation of Garrick Street to the west, into St. Martin's Lane, many of Covent

c*

Garden's slums were swept away. In the very heart of the district, more went when George Peabody, in the mid-nineteenth century, gave his bequest for the building of flats 'to ameliorate the conditions of the poor and needy of this great metropolis and to promote their comfort and happiness'.

With the demolition of the old buildings went much of the material evidence of Covent Garden's history too, but it would be foolish to regret it, for the sum of human misery amongst the poor of Victorian and Edwardian London was immeasurably lessened. The squalor and evil have gone, but the literary glories of Covent Garden live on, in the theatres, the poems, the novels, the essays and the memories of the brilliant men it nourished.

Chapter 5
Bow Street and the Fieldings

BOW STREET was as fashionable as the rest of Covent Garden when it was first built in 1637 – 'Open and large, with very good houses, well inhabited, and resorted unto by gentry for lodgings, as are most of the other streets in this parish,' remarked Strype. Edmund Waller was living here in 1654 when he wrote his eulogy of Oliver Cromwell, who had a house in nearby Long Acre. Wycherley, despite his money troubles, lived on to enjoy many years here, after his jealous first wife died. Robert Harley, Earl of Oxford, was born in Bow Street in 1661 and Grinling Gibbons had a house on the east side, where he lived from 1678 till his death in 1721. Jerry-building was not unknown in the seventeenth century. Grinling Gibbons's house, which cannot have been very old, collapsed while he was living in it and had to be rebuilt. *The Postman* for January 24, 1701 reported: 'On Thursday the house of Mr. Gibbons, the famous carver, in Bow Street, fell down; but by a Special Providence none of the family were killed; but 'tis said that a young girl, which was playing in the court, being missing is supposed to be buried in the rubbish.'

The other illustrious resident during the late seventeenth century was Dr. Radcliffe, whose garden adjoined that of Sir Godfrey Kneller's in the Great Piazza. On the site of the garden, the Floral Hall was to be built. The two were great friends, though they had their squabbles from time to time. Radcliffe was a delightful fellow and a fashionable and highly successful doctor. He is said to have made twenty guineas a day in fees, 'through his vigorous and decisive method of practice, as well as his pleasantry and ready wit; many, it is said, even feigning themselves ill in order to have the pleasure of a few minutes' conversation with him'. When he attended William III he was as frank with him as with his other patients. 'I would not have your Majesty's legs for your three kingdoms,' he exclaimed, examining the King's swollen calves and ankles. He was also physician to Queen Anne, who had had the grace to forgive him after one occasion, before she came to the throne, when he had reported: 'She has only the vapours, and is as well as any woman breathing, if she could only be persuaded to believe it.'

When he died, he left £40,000 for the founding of the magnificent Radcliffe Library at Oxford.

After Rich opened the Covent Garden theatre, one or two taverns and coffee houses frequented by the actors remained fairly exclusive and orderly, but the Bow Street beaux, of whom Dryden had written, no longer continued to live there, for the surrounding courts and alleys became so murky and evil that the street itself began to run down. They have all been swept away now. Helmet Court, Edge Court, Windsor Court and Russell Court with its grim burial ground, and the Star tavern, from where Casanova sent for a number of girls from the surrounding streets, only to find none to his liking, were notorious for their dark deeds. Vinegar Yard, on part of which you stand if you ever wait in the gallery queue for Drury Lane, was as bad – the abode of thieves, prostitutes and unsuccessful authors, some of whom were employed by Curll, the publisher of obscene literature, to write salacious pieces for him. Pope, in his *Instructions how to find Mr. Curll's Authors*, speaks of 'the schoolmaster with carbuncles in his nose, residing at the Hercules and Hell in Vinegar Yard'.

This, then, was Bow Street when Henry Fielding arrived in 1748 with his wife and family and his blind half-brother, John. At that time crime in England, particularly in London, was more rife than it has ever been, before or since. From 1700 to 1800 the population of England and Wales rose from five and a half million to nearly nine million; and in London alone it increased from half a million to one million. What Queen Elizabeth I and James I had feared had come to pass. London had grown too big to be governed efficiently by the old method of unpaid magistrates and voluntary constables.

The upper crust of gentry, wits and gallants, professional people and wealthy tradesmen was very thin, and below it teemed the increasing masses of the poor, many of them unemployed and destitute. In fact, it has been estimated that at the beginning of the eighteenth century a quarter of the population were paupers, illiterate and helpless; and conditions were inevitably worse in the towns and cities, particularly London. The dawning industrial revolution did not help them, and in the filthy and obscene squalor of the London slums they starved and froze and rotted, often resorting to crime through sheer will to keep alive.

It was a cruel and violent age. The Poor Law of 1601 was still in operation, but its administration was corrupt, and even for those who were fortunate enough to receive it, the money served only to keep them barely alive. For wrongdoers the penalties were grim, but desperation usually drove them to take the risks that were involved. As late as 1769 160 offences were listed for which the penalty was death or transportation to the American colonies. They included smuggling, horse and cattle thieving and the stealing of money. There were records of men and women being hanged for stealing no more than 5/–, while for minor offences the penalties were fines, for those who could pay them, the pillory or the stocks. Yet many escaped justice, for there was no proper organization to control or apprehend them, and the less stout-hearted among the poor were too frightened and too anxious for a possible share of the loot to help the cause of the law.

On the lonely country roads, which stretched for miles between isolated towns and villages, highwaymen were such a menace that the guards of stage coaches were always armed, while to travel alone after dark was little short of foolhardiness. The approaches to London were particularly bad. The highwayman Dick Turpin had started his career as a footpad, and in the narrow, unlighted streets of London this was easy enough. Covent Garden was pestered with them and Shenstone, writing during the reign of George II, said: 'London is really dangerous at this time; the pickpockets, formerly contented with mere filching, make no scruple to knock people down with bludgeons in Fleet Street and the Strand, and that at no later hour than eight o'clock at night; but in the Piazzas, Covent Garden, they come in large bodies, armed with couteaus, and attack whole parties, so that the danger of coming out of the playhouses is of some weight in the opposite scale when I am disposed to go to them oftener than I ought.'

The Mohocks were a notorious band of young bloods and bullies who also haunted the London streets at this time. 'These disorderly, ruffians,' wrote Peter Cunningham, 'seldom ventured within the City proper, where the watch was more efficient than in any other parts; but took their stand about St. Clement's Dane and Covent Garden, breaking the watchman's lantern and halberd, and frequently locking him up in his own stand-box.'

England had been mainly a beer-drinking nation until the late seventeenth century, the rich drinking wine and French brandies as well, but when the import duties were imposed on wine and brandy people were permitted, and in fact encouraged, to distil spirits from English corn, which hitherto had been a monopoly of the Distillers' Company and other holders of a royal patent. The result was that gin was manufactured in such vast quantities that very soon there were between 6,000 and 7,000 dram shops in London alone, and the poor found it a cheaper and quicker escape into oblivion than beer. Drunkenness, which stimulated crime, became so widespread and excessive that in 1736 the government imposed a duty of 20/- on every gallon of gin distilled, the first of several efforts they made before the menace was controlled.

People were committed to prison after arrest and often had to wait months for their trials. They were at the mercy of their corrupt gaolers, who were seldom paid but relied on bribes and extortion from their prisoners for their livelihoods. The most monstrous of their practices were the 'gaol' fines, imposed on prisoners who had been found innocent, but which they were forced to pay before they were set free, In the debtors' prisons, men with any money at all were expected to pay for their lodging. Living conditions were appalling and food a bare minimum, prisoners being expected to provide anything better for themselves, usually by bribing the gaolers to buy it for them. Once committed, the debtors remained in prison until their debts were paid, and if there were no one to help them they remained there for the rest of their lives, which were usually cut short by starvation and disease.

Jonathan Wild, the notorious 'Thief-taker in General', on whose character Gay probably based Peachum in his *Beggar's Opera*, earned a living by organizing the theft of people's property and then offering to find it and sell it back to them. He had the audacity to set up his office only a few doors from the Old Bailey. In his early days, he was put into the debtors' prison in Wood Street by his first mistress. She seems to have been the only woman in his life with the wit to get the better of him, and he ended up in the lowest division of that terrible place, the Hole, a room 33 feet by 15 feet, in which seventy men and women were crowded, most of them imprisoned for debt. Here they cooked, ate, lived and slept. The beds were bare boards ranged round the walls in tiers, the highest reached by ladders, and for those who were completely destitute a little bread was provided by charity.

The administration of justice in England was still as it had been since medieval times, by men chosen from amongst the local gentry and appointed by the Crown as unpaid Justices of the Peace, to govern the district in the name of the King. Though nominally they were officials of the State, in practice these appointments were made by the Lord Lieutenants of the Counties. The Justice of the Peace administered either at the Quarter or Petty Sessions or from his own home. He decided on the county rate, where this was levied at all, and was responsible for the maintenance of roads and bridges, prisons and workhouses, the licensing of taverns and the administration of the Poor Law.

However, he had no paid staff to help him. Constables, whose task it was to keep the peace, were ordinary, unpaid citizens, who took yearly terms of office in rotation.

By the eighteenth century, though in country districts men of substance and

An eighteenth-century 'Charlie' or watchman. (Courtesy Metropolitan Police, Bow Street.)

integrity could still be found to spare time to serve honourably on the Bench, it was a very different matter in the towns, particularly in London. Though Justices of the Peace were still unpaid, and it was not till 1792 that the system of stipendiary magistrates was officially introduced, they were entitled to certain fees. Men of lesser calibre, whom Smollett described as 'of profligate lives, needy, mean, ignorant and rapacious', now sometimes bribed their way into being appointed Justices of the Peace, in order to make a living out of the public by extortion and corrupt use of their powers. These 'trading justices' did well for themselves, for the penalties they had the right to enforce were grim enough to warrant the greatest possible financial sacrifices on the part of the prisoners and their friends.

In London, too, the system of voluntary constables who helped the magistrates had broken down, for people had taken to delegating their duties, for a small payment, to men prepared to do the work for a living. As early as Charles II's time, these watchmen, the 'Charlies', had become a recognized institution, though they were, for the most part, far too old for the job and hopelessly ineffectual. 'They were chosen out of those poor, old, decrepit people who are from their want of bodily strength rendered incapable of getting a living by work,' wrote Henry Fielding in *Amelia*. 'These men, armed only with a pole, which some of them are scarce able to lift, are to secure the persons and houses of His Majesty's subjects from the attacks of young, bold, stout, and desperate and well-armed villains . . . If the poor old fellows should run away from such enemies no one, I think, can wonder unless he should wonder that they are able even to make their escape.'

These were the conditions in which Henry and John Fielding had to contend with thieves, prostitutes, procurers, homosexuals, cut-throats, receivers, counterfeiters, swindlers, gamblers, drunkards, dope addicts, and a swarm of miserable, poverty-stricken human beings, who, at the slightest provocation, could be changed by murderous gangs into an hysterical, almost unmanageable rabble.

Henry Fielding was born in 1707 of distinguished parents, the grandson of a Judge of the King's Bench. After leaving Eton, 'uncommonly versed in the Greek authors, and an early master of the Latin classics', he came to London. His father, by no means a rich man, had been widowed and had re-married, and Henry's promised allowance was not forthcoming. Lack of funds did not deter Henry from enjoying life in London. He began to write for the theatre. His first play, dedicated to Lady Mary Wortley Montagu, to whom he was related, was *Love in Several Masques*, performed at Drury Lane in 1728, when he was only 21, and made successful by the brilliant acting of Anne Oldfield. He then went to Leyden University for a while, but a year later he was back in Covent Garden, writing for Drury Lane again. He turned out a quick succession of farces and social satires, which though as bawdy as some of the Restoration comedies, were by no means so successful; but they served to keep him in tolerable comfort. As Lady Mary remarked: 'He would have thrown his work into the fire, if meat could have been got without money, and money without scribbling.' But by now he was married and had responsibilities.

In 1737 he was admitted to the Middle Temple for three years, and was called to the Bar in 1740. He published his first novel, *Joseph Andrews*, and continued to make a little money from his plays. Garrick produced *The Wedding Day* in 1743, with Peg Woffington as his leading lady. Shortly afterwards came his *Life of Jonathan Wild*, and then he set to work on his masterpiece, *Tom Jones*.

In 1748, still poor, he was appointed by the Duke of Bedford, shortly after the death of Sir Thomas de Veil, to succeed him as magistrate and principal justice of Westminster and Middlesex. Not many years before his death, De Veil had taken a house in Bow Street, from which he administered his offices. Here the Fieldings, with Henry's half-brother, John, who had been blind from birth, established themselves. Henry's district extended over the parishes of St. Paul's, Covent Garden, St. Martin-in-the-Fields and St. George's, Bloomsbury.

His fees were said to amount to £1,000 a year, but Fielding wrote: 'I had reduced an income of about £500 a year of the dirtiest money upon earth to little more than £300; a considerable portion of which remained with my clerk; and indeed if the whole had done so as it ought, he would be but ill-paid for sitting almost 16 hours in the 24 in the most nauseous as well as unwholesome air in the universe, which hath in his case corrupted a good constitution without contaminating his morals.'

Fielding was soon hard at work, sometimes making fifty commitments a week. A few months later he was writing that 'having received information that a large number of people were at a gambling house in the Strand, he sent for a party of soldiers from the Tilt Yard to aid the constables in arresting them; and it took till two a.m. to examine the 45 accused.' Within a year or two, his blind brother, John, became his assistant. Fielding's ability was soon recognized and in May, 1749 he was elected chairman of the Quarter Sessions for the City and Liberty of Westminster.

Despite the labours of Henry and John, crime in London seemed unabated, and at last, at the time of the publication of Henry's *Enquiry in to the Causes of the Late Increase of Robbers*, officialdom showed practical interest in helping them. A commission was appointed and the government offered a reward of £100 for any criminals apprehended. People who had been victims of a robbery had hitherto been in the habit of themselves offering a reward for the recovery of their property, with no questions asked; a habit which played magnificently into the hands of rogues like Jonathan Wild. This was now made illegal, victims being instructed to pass all the information on to the Fieldings at their Bow Street office.

Henry Fielding was granted enough money to secure the part-time services of eighty constables, for whom he drew up rules of conduct and procedure. The Gin Act of 1751, by limiting the sale of gin and once more increasing its price, considerably reduced the drunkenness, which Fielding had for long declared was one of the prime causes of the trouble. Nevertheless, the crime situation remained appallingly bad, and after an outbreak of particularly vicious murders in 1753, the Duke of Newcastle asked him to prepare a new plan for dealing with the problem. Henry Fielding was a sick man and his days were numbered. He submitted his scheme, which was to develop into the organization of the Bow Street Runners, but was not to live to see it in operation. He was forced to resign, handing over the work to John, and in the autumn of 1754 he died, at the age of 47.

John, who was knighted six years later, set to work. With a grant from the Exchequer he organized six officers, who were the first Bow Street Runners. They were renowned for their skill in solving difficult cases and apprehending the culprits, and were prepared to travel all over the country, when other police offices asked for their help. In addition, John Fielding had a patrol of 68 men, divided into 13 parties, each consisting of a captain and four or five men, who patrolled the streets of the neighbourhood at night and also appeared at public processions and any other large gatherings where there might be outbreaks of disorder. The men were armed with cutlasses, and the captains each carried a brace of pistols as well.

In the early days they did not wear uniform, but in the early nineteenth century, after Sir John's time, the Horse Patrol was formed to control the highways against a fresh outbreak of highway robbery. They were put into a uniform of blue coat, scarlet waistcoat, blue trousers, Wellington boots, black leather hat and blue greatcoat. The Bow Street men were then similarly equipped, and earned the name of the Robin Redbreasts.

Sir John was given two assistant magistrates. He ruled at Bow Street till 1780, a wise and kindly man who overcame his disability with remarkable skill and courage. It is interesting to read in *The Gentleman's Magazine* for September 15, 1773 that: 'This day Sir John Fielding informed the bench of justices that he had last year written to Mr. Garrick concerning the impropriety of performing *The Beggar's Opera*, which never was represented on the stage without creating an additional number of real thieves; he begged, therefore, the gentlemen present would join with him in requesting Mr. Garrick from performing that opera on Saturday evening. The bench immediately consented to the proposal; and a polite note was despatched to Mr. Garrick for that purpose.'

Garrick replied with equal courtesy, but pointed out, quite firmly, the difficulties of altering his programme at such short notice. No hard feelings were permanently felt, for when Garrick retired from the stage a few years later, Sir John sent him a warm tribute, to which Garrick replied with equal charm. 'No one is more sensible of Sir John Fielding's merit, nor has more publicly declared it,' wrote Garrick, and added that he would be 'more cheerful if Sir John will come and dine occasionally.'

This was about the time that Sir John was dealing with that extraordinary character Charlie Price, the swindler and forger, who made up in ingenuity what he lacked in moral fibre. At one time he was running, with his current mistress, a bogus matrimonial agency in Southampton Street, advertising in the newspaper:

'To gentlemen of character, fortune and honour who wish to engage for life with a lady who possesses the above qualities in a very eminent degree. Her person in point of elegance, gives precedence to none. Her mind and manners are highly cultivated, her temper serene, mild and affable, and her age does not exceed 22. Any gentleman who answers the above address may direct a letter to A.Z., at the Bedford Head, Southampton Street, Strand; and if their morals and situation in life are approved, they will then be waited on by a person who will procure the parties an interview.'

One gullible young man paid fifty guineas for the privilege of an interview with the young paragon's guardian, who was none other than Charlie in heavy disguise, but waited in vain for a glimpse of his bride.

A few years later, Charlie was raising money to open a brewery, which never materialized, and then he ran a bogus lottery office in King Street for a while. He filled in his time making forged bank notes, but these were his final undoing. He was caught and committed to prison, but hanged himself in his cell before he could be brought to trial.

The year of Sir John's death, 1780, saw the outbreak of the Gordon riots, when the mob, after releasing the prisoners of Newgate and attacking the Old Bailey, burnt down the Fleet and the King's Bench prisons, made an attempt to break into the Bank of England, and swarmed into Bow Street, setting fire to the police court and gutting the ground floor. Sir John, already in failing health, was not there at the time, but one of his assistants, who was to become his successor, Sir William Addington, was in charge and sent for help from the militia.

The house was rebuilt and was to hear many strange cases, the oddest of them all probably being the sad affair of Mr. Hill and Miss Johnston.

'A whimsical investigation took place before Mr. Graham in Bow Street on Saturday last,' ran the report. 'It was a kind of double charge; the first made on the part of Mr. Arthur Hill, of Carburton Street, against a Miss Alice Johnston, a Titchfield Street belle, for pulling off one of his *whiskers*, which happened to be one of the *false* kind, in the coffee room of the Covent Garden theatre. The second, instituted by the lady, *viz.* that in consequence of this accidental derangement of the whisker, Mr. Arthur Hill caught her in his arms and by a malicious dexterity let her so far slide through her clothes as to make that sort of public exhibition which even shocked the circle of spectators who are pretty well accustomed to *strange sights!* Mr. Hill, who had previously spent the night coolly in the watch-house, being called upon for his defence justified his plea on the ground of *retaliation;* the magistrate holding that the former was rather an accidental assault, and that in the latter there was nothing to stir up His Majesty's liege subjects to any breach of the *peace* – although evidently a shameful breach of decorum, dismissed the parties with a reprimand and an exhortation to better manners.'[1]

But what an end to an evening which may well have begun with such high hopes!

The Bow Street Runners, who operated for nearly seventy years until the formation of Sir Robert Peel's police force, were concerned with the apprehension and detection of crime, rather than its prevention. They were, in fact, a special branch, in addition to the mounted and foot patrols which, during the latter part of the eighteenth century, were coming into operation at police offices all over the country.

At no time were there more than twelve Bow Street Runners; normally there were only eight. Their insignia of office was a small baton, surmounted by a gilt crown, and, like the patrols, they were armed.

In 1828, when the chief clerk of Bow Street was giving his report to a House of Commons committee, he said that of the eight principal Bow Street Runners attached to the office at that time, 'Townsend and Sayer generally attended his Majesty when he was out of town. They are now at Brighton. Salmon and Ruthven have been upon the continent in pursuit of persons who have absconded with property belonging to their employers in the city. They are both returned. Bishop has been at a variety of places in the country – I think three or four places – on business. Taunton has been to the assizes. A little while before that he followed some offenders to Scotland, and brought them from thence. Vickery has been employed a good deal in making inquiries for the post-office, relative to some offences that have been committed there . . . Smith has been employed in a variety of matters in Kent and Essex, and at Norwich, and latterly at Baldock in Hertfordshire. In fact, when they are not called out of town to attend to offences committed in the country, they devote their time and attention to the discharge of their duties in London.'

[1]Quoted in *The History of the Bow Street Runners* by Gilbert Armitage.

There seem to have been few rules about their duties, and when they were not away on special investigations they attended race meetings, the theatre bars and any other crowded functions where criminals might be found. One of them was always at Court, guarding the members of the royal family.

The most famous of the runners was Townsend, who was often detailed to guard King George III. He seems to have been a shrewd and jovial character, though probably also a wicked old scrounger.

'This man, who was said to have commenced life as a costermonger, became by effrontery and impudence, enhanced by a certain share of low cunning and low wit, the head of his profession,' wrote one Richardson, who obviously thought little of him. 'He derived a large income from the Christmas boxes of the nobility and of other parties at whose routs he was employed to detect, or keep away, improper characters, who, he persuaded his patrons, would be present if *he* were not in attendance. As to his personal appearance, he was a very smart little man, clean as paint, to use his own phrase, and I think peculiar in his costume. He was generally encased in a light and loud suit, knee-breeches, and short gaiters, and a white hat of great breadth of brim . . . At his death it was reported that he had made accumulations from the guinea a day at the bank, the nobility, the money from prosecutions, etc. to the amount of £20,000. He was often seen in familiar conversation with George III, whose good-humoured face was convulsed with laughter at his stories.'

Townsend was an extremely active officer, and it was said that 'his name alone became a terror to the wicked and abandoned part of the community'; but amongst the fashionable society of London 'knowing Townsend' became a cult. Sometimes the note 'Mr. Townsend will attend' was even added to the announce-ment of a rout or ball, as a kind of added attraction. There is no doubt that the fuss and flattery all went to his head a little. We are told that 'the artful fellow, to increase his imposture, would, in particular crowds, caution noble ladies to be on their guard, and they would hand over their watches and jewellery on the spot to Mr. Townsend's kind and safe keeping. In the restoration of the articles it was equally the fashion to remunerate Mr. Townsend for his thoughtfulness and trouble'.

He became, not surprisingly, a shocking snob. 'Bless you, sir,' the old man said one day, when he was reminiscing, 'I knew the opera fifty years ago, and then it was worthy of being called a King's Theatre, for only the nobility had boxes; but now you may see a duchess on one side and a wholesale cheesemonger's wife on the other. I remember the time when there were masquerades, too, and the king – God bless him! – (he was only Prince of Wales then) used to have nice freaks on such occasions. Many a time I have taken him by the skirt of the coat when he was going in, and said to him, I would advise your Royal Highness, if you have got any money on you, to leave it with me for safety; and then he would pull out a purse with fifty or sixty guineas in it, and say, "Well, but Townsend, you must allow me something to spend, you know", and upon that I used to hand him over about five guineas, keeping the rest and his watch in my own pocket, where few people would have thought of looking for them.'

The pay of the Runners was 25/– a week, but when they were called on special duties, the people who had asked for them had to pay their travelling expenses and a guinea a day for their services, while work at Court and at the Pavilion at Brighton earned extra pay. It was customary to give awards to the courts after a conviction for felony, of which the Runners received their share. It was a practice which must almost inevitably lead to corruption, and the people whose property had been recovered were also expected to reward handsomely.

Townsend, in explaining to the House of Commons committee this system of rewards, said: 'The usual way in distributing the £40 on conviction is that the recorder gives the prosecutor from £5 to £15 and £20, according to the circumstances, and the apprehender the remainder; that comes to, perhaps, only £3 or £4 apiece . . .'

Another way of making money was by the distribution of Tyburn tickets, the possession of one of these tickets exempting the holder from having to perform the voluntary guard duties which were expected of every worthy citizen. The highest price for a Tyburn ticket was, according to Townsend, paid by the residents of Covent Garden, where the current value was £25 . . .'For the constable of the parish must sit up, I think, one night out of three; and whoever is hit upon as a parochial constable says, "This is a hard thing, and therefore I will buy myself off"; and a ticket in that parish, therefore, is worth more.' Townsend went on to say that: 'If an officer gets a guinea a day, it is a chance whether he gets any reward; that must depend upon the liberality of those public offices who choose to pay it', and added, tendentiously, 'I am very sorry to say that sometimes they are rather mean upon that subject.'

However, the Bow Street Runners did do some very useful and skilful detective work, in the course of which they frequently ran into great personal danger. Vickery became renowned for his skill in catching French prisoners who broke their parole and tried to escape. He also traced two men who, by a trick, had stolen £35,000 worth of jewellery from a shop in Ludgate Hill. He followed them through France and Holland to Frankfurt and managed to recover £20,000 worth of the property.

Donaldson specialized in apprehending pickpockets who haunted the saloons at the Covent Garden and Drury Lane theatres. From time to time he used to call out: 'Take care of your pockets!'

'Most persons considered this exclamation as a warning to the unwary,' observed the cynical Mr. Richardson. 'Others, less charitably inclined, affirmed that it was a notice given to the pickpockets to be on the look-out, and take heed who the gentlemen were, who immediately put their hands in their pockets to ascertain that the contents were safe, and thus furnished the thieves with a clue to where they could go to work with the greatest chance of success.'

Coleman, the last counterfeiter to be executed in this country, was caught by another famous Bow Street officer, Keys. Keys knew Coleman by sight and was practically certain of the street where he lived, though not the house, and he wanted to catch him in the actual act of counterfeiting. Coleman, who was selling his faked shillings at 4/– for twenty, was extremely careful, never leaving his house if he saw a stranger about in the street and never carrying his counterfeit coins on his person, but using a small girl to follow him, carrying them in a basket.

Keys employed a man, at 3/6 a day, to disguise himself as a milkman with his yoke of pails over his shoulders, and walk through the street three times a day. The man knew what Coleman looked like and he kept watch for close on two months, with no result. At last he told Keys he felt he was wasting his time, but Keys would not give in, knowing that the more familiar the figure of the milkman became, the less likely Coleman was to consider him. Keys' patience was rewarded. One morning Coleman looked out into the street, saw only the innocuous, familiar figure of the milkman and came out to feed his chickens. The milkman duly noted the house and reported to Keys, who that night, with some members of the patrol to support him, called on Coleman. 'When I got to the top of the stairs,' said Keys, 'I could hear Jem and his woman, Rhoda Coleman, as she was called, conversing about the coin while working. "That's a rum 'un, Rhoda," said Jem.'

'I was about to break the door in with my foot,' continued Keys, 'in fact, I had lifted my leg up, and had placed my back against the opposite wall for that purpose, when I heard Coleman say, "Rhoda, go and get us a quartern of gin." I waited about two minutes, and she opened the door to go out for the gin. I and my comrades rushed in and secured Coleman with the moulds and work red-hot in his hands, He was surprised, but cool. "Do yer want me, master?" said he, looking up in my face. "Of course I do, Jem," said I; and having hand-cuffed him, I proceeded to search the place. We took away upwards of £20 worth of counterfeit coin, as well as all the implements, etc. used in the process of manufacturing it.' Coleman was tried, convicted and executed, but Rhoda was acquitted. Keys said that she 'removed the body to her lodgings, and kept it for 12 days. I had information three times that if I went I should find Rhoda coining again, and that the moulds, etc. were concealed in the coffin, under the body of poor Jem Coleman. This, I afterwards ascertained, was the fact.'[2]

In 1825 a new police court was built in Bow Street on the west side, almost opposite the Fieldings' old house, but it was only three years later than the Runners were pensioned off and superseded by the new police force. The new court was described as a commodious room with a bar across its midst. 'Behind the bar, at a table, sits the Magistrate, attired in a Court suit of the days of Goldsmith, and girt with a sword. By his side sits his "clerke", occupied in the "reduction" of the depositions, and clad in a gorgeous periwig. The prisoner is guarded by a couple of Bow-street "Runners", and the general public is represented by some dozen or so of fashionably-attired ladies and gentlemen, who are strolling about and exchanging snuff and pomander boxes, and watching the proceedings with a languid interest.'

However, by 1881 it had become a grim and evil place, 'the general air of greasiness and of dirt which hung about it stifling the faculties and perceptions of all who were engaged in its business, from the Chief Magistrate himself down to the door-keeper.'‡

That year it was abandoned for the present, rather awe-inspiring building, back on the east side of the street, which today is the scene of the first hearing of so many modern crimes.

[2]Quoted in *Chronicles of Bow Street Police-Office* by Percy Fitzgerald, Chapman and Hall, 1888.
‡*ibid.*

Chapter 6
St. Paul's Church

INIGO JONES'S church of St. Paul has suffered many changes in its 300-odd years of history. When the Earl of Bedford ordered it to be built, it was rather through necessity, to provide a place of worship for his new tenants. He was running out of money. 'In short,' he said to Inigo Jones, 'I would have it not much better than a barn.' 'Well, then, you shall have the handsomest barn in England,' replied Inigo Jones. And at a cost of £4,500 he built the charming little red brick church, with its simple Tuscan portico on to the main square and its entrance leading into the small churchyard to the west, its gently sloping roof and widely overhanging eaves. On the north, the churchyard is flanked by the backs of the houses in King Street and on the south by those of Henrietta Street. From both of these streets the churchyard can be reached by small tunnel entrances, built under the first floors of the houses. The main entrance to the churchyard gives on to Inigo Place, which opens on to Bedford Street.

Inside the entrance is a wide vestibule, with stairs on the left leading up to the organ gallery. To the right of the vestibule is a large vestry, to the left the Rector's vestry, in which the Church records are carefully preserved.

The central door in the vestibule leads to the Church itself, simple and dignified, with its white walls, tall, rounded-arched windows and austere altar, behind which are four carved wooden pilasters and a triangular pediment in harmony with the eastern portico. The carved oak pulpit, with its gilded angels, stands on the nothern side of the main aisle, and the organ gallery is over the western entrance.

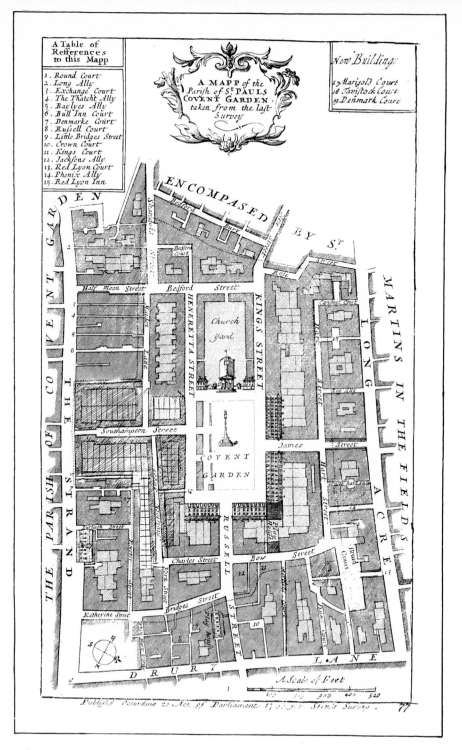

Map of Covent Garden in 1755, from Stow's Survey. (Courtesy Covent Garden Market Authority.)

The ceiling, now ornamented with plaster work, was once painted, but apart from this there were few other embellishments and no pillars. It was, in truth, as plain as a barn, but beautiful in its light and proportions and homely plainness.

During the years of the Commonwealth, there was a good deal of interference in the conduct of the services of the Church of England. Evelyn records how, while attending Christmas morning service at the chapel of Exeter House, close by in the Strand, 'when the service was ended, and the Sacrament about to be administered, the chapel was surrounded by soldiers, and all the communicants and assembly surprised and kept prisoners. As we went up to receive the Sacrament, the miscreants held their muskets against us, as if they would have shot us at the altar, but yet suffering us to finish the office of Communion, as perhaps not having instructions what to do in case they found us in that action.'

Evelyn was imprisoned in a room in Exeter House for a few hours, and later in the day examined by several officers as to why 'contrary to an ordinance made, that none should any longer observe the superstitious time of the Nativity, I durst offend. Finding no colour to detain me, they dismissed me with every pity of my ignorance.'

There is no record of any such interference with the worshippers at St. Paul's, but they seem to have been Royalist in their sympathies. When Charles I was executed, his statue in Whitehall was removed and handed over to a brazier named Rivett, to be destroyed. He managed to conceal it in the vaults of St. Paul's, and in order to give the impression that he had melted it down, made a number of small bronzes – figures and vases – which he sold as relics of the original statue. After the Restoration, the statue was brought out again and re-erected in its old position.

Horace Walpole did not care for the appearance of St. Paul's. 'The arcade of Covent Garden and the church – two structures of which I want taste to see the beauties,' he wrote. 'In the arcade there is nothing remarkable; the pilasters are as errant and homely stripes as any plasterer would make. The barn roof over the portico of the church strikes my eyes with as little idea of dignity or beauty as it could do if it covered nothing but a barn. In justice to Inigo, one must own that the defect is not in the architect, but in the order; who ever saw a beautiful Tuscan building? Would the Romans have chosen that order for a temple?' But then Walpole's fancy was more florid, and if his Gothic castle at Strawberry Hill is any criterion, many of us want taste to see beauty where he himself found it.

For 100 years after its dedication the congregations of St. Paul's were large and fashionable. They were soon adding embellishments to their church, which later generations deplored and removed. During the plague, when so many left

London for the country, the Rector of St. Paul's, Simon Patrick, stayed at his post, selflessly ministering to the sick and dying, and blessing the dead at their mass funerals. When his friends warned him of his danger and begged him to leave, he replied: 'What! Am I better than another? I must stay with my charge.' His only recorded complaint is that, while burying the dead at night, he 'found the autumn winds prejudicial'.

In 1727 the portico had to be restored. Sixty years later some of the plaster work was replaced by stone facing and the brick and plaster porches rebuilt in Portland stone. Then, in 1795, the church suffered a disastrous fire. The roof and painted ceiling and parts of the walls were destroyed. The Lely portrait of Charles I was lost, as well as the memorial statute to Lely himself, with the Grinling Gibbons bust. However, the records were saved and also the pulpit, attributed to Gibbons or one of his pupils. Plans were quickly made for the re-building of the church. Once more the question of its stark simplicity was raised, and some wanted a change, but the architect, Hardwick, remained faithful to Inigo's original conception and reproduced it truthfully.

By this time, the congregations were dwindling, for the Garden was no longer so fashionable. Then, as time moved into the nineteenth century, it was felt that something must be done about the crowded graveyard, where so many people, some illustrious, not a few infamous, had by now been buried. In fact nowhere, probably in the whole of London, apart from Westminster Abbey and St. Paul's Cathedral, had so many famous people been laid to rest. Here lay actors and playwrights, poets and writers, philosophers and musicians, representing all that was best in English literature, drama, music and painting of the late seventeenth and the eighteenth centuries.

However, the practical Victorians decided that the churchyard was full enough. Someone described it as a 'plague-spot of human flesh and human remains; the narrow place of sepulchre of two centuries of the inhabitants of this parish'. In 1853 the burial ground was closed, and two years later the tombstones were removed and used to pave the paths of the memorial garden which has taken its place. The passage of feet has worn away most of the inscriptions now, but sometimes, as you walk there, the sunlight gives a glimpse of a long-forgotten name or a fading date, which will make you pause awhile and tread softly.

The church records reflect not only the history of the Garden but of England itself. One of the first men to be buried here was Robert Carr, a favourite of James I, who had been living in a house on the north side of Russell Street, and who died in 1645. His name is associated with the worst scandal of the reign. His closest friend was the young poet, Sir Thomas Overbury. The two were inseparable till they met and both fell in love with the young, beautiful but unscrupulously wicked Countess of Essex, who, against her will, had been married to the son of Queen Elizabeth's Earl of Essex.

It was Carr whom the Countess favoured, and for him she sought an annulment of her marriage with the young Essex. Thomas Overbury, perhaps through jealousy, perhaps, having come to know the Countess too well, through sincere regard for his old friend, opposed the match and hinted that he knew of reasons why the Essex marriage could not be broken. The Countess, furious that anyone should attempt to thwart her plans, contrived to bring disgrace on Sir Thomas, so that he was arrested and confined in the Tower.

It may very well have been while he was in prison here that he wrote his poem *The Wife*, the first verse of which gives the young man's general opinion of womankind.

> Each woman is a *briefe* of Womankind,
> And doth in little even as much containe
> As in one Day and Night all life we find,
> Of either more is but the same againe;
> > *God* fram'd Her so that to her *HUSBAND* She
> > As *Eve* should all the *World of Woman be*.

Be that as it may, the Countess now began proceedings for the annulment of her marriage. They were successful, but a few days before she was free to marry Carr, Sir Thomas died in the Tower, suddenly and mysteriously.

Three months later, Carr, by now become the Earl of Somerset, was married to his Countess, but people did not forget the young and elegant Sir Thomas. Rumours and gossip spread. People who had known and loved Sir Thomas declared that he had died in physical agony. At last, the talk could no longer be ignored. Carr and his wife were arrested, charged with the murder of Sir Thomas by slow poisoning. Witnesses attested to Sir Thomas's sufferings before his death and the Carrs and their accomplices were found guilty. The accomplices were duly hanged, but Carr, alleged to be only an accessory after the fact, was pardoned and set free, while his wife, instead of being condemned to the gallows along with the people she had egged on to commit the crime, was retained in prison in relative comfort. Two years later, she, too, was set free. Royal patronage, it seemed, had given them protection; but their erstwhile friends and the rest of the world never forgave them. Henceforth society shunned the Somersets, and for the rest of their lives the gates of their mansion were seldom opened to receive visitors. The couple ended by hating each other. Carr lived on for another thirty unhappy years, and his only daughter married the Earl of Bedford, who laid out the square. Thus it happened that he came to be buried in St. Paul's churchyard.

Three years later, in 1648, from his home on the west side of James Street near the corner of Hart Street, there came for his burial Sir Henry Herbert, brother of Lord Herbert of Cherbury and George Herbert. Sir Henry had been one of the last to hold the Court office of Master of the Revels.

Claude Duval, the highwayman, was a Frenchman who came to England as a valet shortly after the Restoration. He soon took to the road, leading a gang of robbers who haunted the northern approaches of London, particularly Holloway, between Islington and Highgate.

Macaulay tells how 'at the head of his troop, he stopped a lady's coach, in which there was a booty of £400; how he took only £100, and suffered the fair owner to ransom the rest by dancing a coranto with him on the heath'. True or not, it was a good story which fired the imaginations of the romantically-minded young women who had not suffered from his attentions, though the few who had been his victims may have felt less well-disposed towards him. Nevertheless, when in 1669, at the age of 27, Claude Duval was at last captured at Mother Maberley's tavern, The-Hole-In-The-Wall in Chandos Street, then brought to his trial and hanged at Tyburn, there was much lamentation. His body was cut down and brought to the Tangier tavern in St. Giles's for a 'lying-in-state'. Then he was given a splendid funeral at St. Paul's, attended with flambeaux and followed by a long train of mourners, 'to the great grief of the women'. He is said to have been buried under the central aisle of the church, with an epitaph which ran:

Here lies Duval, Reader, if male thou art
Look to thy purse, if female, to thy heart.

But there is no trace of that epitaph today and they say that his body was long ago taken away to some unknown spot for fresh burial.

Samuel Butler, who in 1680 died of consumption at his lodging in Rose Street, and whose friends could not afford to give him a funeral at Westminster Abbey, was buried, according to his own request, close to the west front of St. Paul's. The same year Sir Peter Lely was buried there, and nine years later we read of the baptism of the infant daughter of the future Duke and Duchess of Kingston, who herself was to become the distinguished Lady Mary Wortley Montagu. She was born too early to become a member of the Blue Stocking Club, but she was a strong protagonist of women's rights. In particular, she insisted on the need for proper education for girls and on their freedom to marry whom they pleased, instead of submitting to the arranged and usually loveless marriages which the aristocracy of the time were in the habit of negotiating for their daughters.

'I am inclined to think that Nature has not placed us in an inferior rank to men, no more than females of other animals, she wrote. 'We are educated in the grossest ignorance, and no art omitted to stifle our natural reason.' Lady Mary was a rebel. While still a child, she taught herself Latin, 'by the help of an uncommon memory and indefatigable labour', for she had been left in the charge of an old governess, who 'though perfectly good and pious, wanted capacity'.

Later, in defiance of her father's wishes, she made a runaway marriage with Edward Wortley Montagu. Many years later we find her writing to her daughter, the Countess of Bute, on the same theme of education for girls, this time in regard to her own small grand-daughter. 'Learning,' she said, 'if she has a real taste for it, will not only make her contented, but happy in it. No entertainment is so cheap as reading, nor any pleasure so lasting.' However, bearing in mind the persistent prejudice against women with intellects, she shrewdly advises the small girl to 'conceal whatever learning she attains, with as much solicitude as she would hide crookedness or lameness . . .'

Dick Estcourt, the greatly loved actor from Drury Lane, and the handsome Edward Kynaston, whom Pepys had so admired, were both buried in St. Paul's churchyard in 1712. Pepys first saw Kynaston acting the part of the Duke's sister in Beaumont and Fletcher's *The Loyal Subject*, declaring that he 'made the loveliest lady that ever I saw in my life, only her voice not very good'. A few months later, he saw him in Ben Jonson's *The Silent Woman* and wrote that 'Kynaston, the boy, had the good turn to appear in three shapes: first, as a poor woman in ordinary clothes, to please Morose; then in fine clothes, as a gallant, and in them was clearly the prettiest woman in the whole house, and lastly, as a man; and then likewise did appear the handsomest man in the house.'

Three years later, it was time for the burying of gay old William Wycherley, from his house in Bow Street, mourned by his new bride of a few days and by many others, too, for he was always a good friend. Even the caustically critical Pope, nearly half a century younger than Wycherley, was one of his greatest admirers. 'The love of some things rewards itself, as of Virtue and of Mr. Wycherley,' he wrote, and on another occasion he declared that Wycherley 'never did an unjust thing to me in his whole life'.

In 1717 another distinguished Covent Garden parishioner, the artist Pierre Tempest, who painted *The Cries of London*, was buried at St. Paul's, and three years later saw the burial of a mysterious young woman, listed as the 'Unknown Lady'. The story goes that she was 'middle-sized, with dark brown hair, and very beautiful features, and the mistress of every accomplishment of fashion', who had arrived from Mansfield to live in Covent Garden in 1714. 'Her circumstances, says Mr. Timbs, in his *Romance of London*, 'were affluent, and she possessed many rich trinkets set with diamonds. A Mr. John Ward, of Hackney, published several particulars of her in the newspapers, and amongst others, said a servant had been directed by her to deliver him a letter after her death; but, as no servant appeared, he felt himself required to notice these circumstances, in order to acquaint her relations that her death occurred suddenly, after a masquerade, where she declared that she had conversed with the king; and it was remembered that she had been seen in the private apartments of Queen Anne, though, after the queen's death, she lived in obscurity.'

The mystery has never been solved, but it has been conjectured that 'she was the daughter of a Roman Catholic who had consigned her to a convent,' says Timbs.

The following year, Grinling Gibbons, who had done so much for Covent Garden and its church, was buried here, and two years afterwards Mrs. Centilivre, that competent dramatist whose name is hardly known today, but whose work during the eighteenth century was often performed, particularly *The Wonder*. Kitty Clive and David Garrick used to play together in this, and both of them chose it for their farewell performances.

Robert Wilks, the actor who built the house next to Convent Garden theatre, where later Macklin, Garrick and Peg Woffington were to set up their stormy household for a while, was buried at St. Paul's in 1732. Twenty years later came a record of the lamentable story of Fielding's 'incomparable Betty Careless', who, in her heyday, had been a highly successful prostitute, though she fell on hard times and died penniless. At least she achieved an obituary notice in the *Gentleman's Magazine*, which in April, 1752 announced: 'Was buried from the Poor-house of St. Paul's, Covent Garden, the famed Betty Careless, who had helped the gay gentlemen of this country to squander £50,000.'

In 1775 the parents of William Turner carried him to his baptism at St. Paul's from their barber's shop in Maiden Lane, little thinking that, 84 years later, he would be buried in the crypt of St. Paul's Cathedral. Turner never married, but after his parents' death he lived a double life, a bachelor existence in Queen Anne Street alternating with a domestic life, under the name of Booth, with a woman friend in Cheyne Walk, in whose house he would sit for hours, watching the sun and sky over the river at dawn and sunset.

Both of Turner's parents were buried at St. Paul's, and in 1778 came Dr. Arne, who had been baptized there in 1710 and spent all his life round and about Covent Garden. His memorial plaque, on the north wall of the church, bears the opening phrase of his best known song, *Rule Brittania*, and beneath it is carved the quotation from Ecclesiastes: 'Let us praise famous men . . . such as found out musical tunes.'

Tom Davies, the famous bookseller and friend of Dr. Johnson, was given a grave here, and in 1797 poor old Charles Macklin ended his long, tempestuous life at last and was buried in the church itself, far up under the nave. His memorial tablet on the south wall reads:

> Sacred to the memory of
> CHARLES MACKLIN
> Comedian
> THIS TABLET IS ERECTED
> (with the aid of public patronage)
> By his affectionate widow Eliz. Macklin
> Obit 11 July, 1797, aetatis 107

That extraordinary character John Wolcot, who wrote under the name of Peter Pindar, was also a Covent Garden man. He lived in Tavistock Row, which is now part of the market, on the north side of Tavistock Street, from 1783 to 1805. He was born in Devonshire in 1738, and took a doctor's degree at Aberdeen, after which he went to Jamaica with Sir William Trelawney for a while as his medical adviser. To fill in time between these not very onerous duties he was ordained and took a church. However, his congregation, mostly negroes, were by no means appreciative of his ministrations, and on the occasions when not one of them appeared for morning service, Wolcot and his clerk would stroll on the seashore and amuse themselves by shooting ring-tailed pigeons. When Trelawney died, Wolcot came back to England and established himself as a doctor in Truro. Here he met the young artist Opie, 'the Cornish boy in tin-mines bred', and recognizing his talents, encouraged and helped him all he could. When he thought he was sufficiently experienced, though the boy was still only 19, he brought him to London. Wolcot had already begun his satirical writings, and Opie seems to have copied his friend and benefactor in the general style of his manner and speech. Distinguished and gifted artist as he was to become, he was usually too abrupt and caustic to please his clients. It was Opie who, when asked by a client how he mixed his colours, replied sharply, 'With brains, sir'.

Now, from his lodgings in Covent Garden, Wolcot began to pour forth a ceaseless stream of brilliant but extremely unmannerly satirical odes, which made him one of the best-hated men of his day. He sneered mercilessly at Boswell:

> Oh, Boswell, Bozzy, Bruce, whate'er thy name,
> Thou mighty shark for anecdote and fame;
> A tomtit twittering on an eagle's back.

In *Peeps at St. James's* he made fun of George III. He belittled the travels of Sir Joseph Banks and also of Sir James Bruce, who had quite enough to endure anyway, when people in England at first refused to believe the accounts of his amazing adventures in eighteenth-century Abyssinia. Even Pitt himself did not escape the Peter Pindar lampoons, and the government was driven, though with ill-success, to try and bribe him to keep silent. Nothing could stem his vitriolic attacks on the famous people of his time, not even blindness in his later years, and increasing illness. He died at his house in Somers Town in 1819, but was brought back to St. Paul's, Covent Garden, to be buried in a vault in the churchyard close to the grave of Samuel Butler.

There were several strange inscriptions on the tombstones of the churchyard, which have long since disappeared.

> Good Friend, for Jesus Sake forebear
> To dig the Dust enclosed here.
> Blest be the Man that spares these Stones,
> And cursed be he that moves my Bones

is an interesting one, as it is, of course, identical with that on Shakespeare's tomb at Stratford.

Mr. Button, of Button's coffee house, was treated to:

> Odds fish, and fiery coals,
> Are graves become Button-holes!

Of all the marriages which have taken place at St. Paul's, perhaps that of Lady Susan Fox-Strangeways to the actor O'Brien of Drury Lane theatre, in 1764, caused most consternation in London society. People raised their hands in dismay that a member of the aristocracy should have so demeaned herself, and Walpole wrote to the Earl of Hertford that the bride's father, Lord Ilchester, 'was almost distracted – even a footman were preferable; the publicity of the hero's profession perpetuates the mortification. I could not have believed Lady Susan would have stooped so low.'

Despite the distinction achieved by Sheridan, who was also a member of Parliament for Westminster for some years, of Garrick, Mrs. Siddons and the Kembles, there is no doubt that the general run of theatre folk were for long considered as 'rogues and vagabonds', and it was not till the present century that their status improved. Then Henry Irving, the first actor to receive a knighthood, writing in 1901, was able to say: 'Today we find the stage recruited by a constant influx from the educated classes'.

During the eighteenth century, Moll King's disreputable coffee house was a ramshackle place built actually against the eastern portico of the church. Here

98

might be found 'the bucks, bloods, demireps, and choice spirits of London, associated with the most elegant and fascinating Cyprians, congregated with every species of human kind that intemperance, idleness, necessity, or curiosity, could assemble together . . . The eminent, the eccentric, and the notorious in every walk of life, were to be found nightly indulging their festivities within its famous precincts . . . Moll King would serve chimney-sweeps, gardeners, and the market-people in common with her lords of the highest rank.' And to add to the confusion of worthier and more soberminded visitors to Covent Garden, 'the front windows of the bagnios under the Piazza were filled from seven at night until four or five o'clock in the morning, with courtesans of every description, who, in the most impudent manner, invited the passengers from the theatres into the houses, where they were accommodated with suppers and lodging, and frequently at the risk of all they possessed'.

However, shortly after her conviction, Moll King retired to the respectability of Hampstead, became a regular church-goer, and died, presumably in a state of grace, in 1747. Her coffee house was pulled down, and by the end of the century the square was more tolerable.

The eastern portico of the church was for many years used as the hustings for the Westminster elections. Elections, before the Reform Bill of 1832, were full-blooded, riotous affairs, perhaps the most exciting of all taking place in Covent Garden in May of 1784, when Sir Cecil Wray and his Tory supporters were making a desperate effort against Charles James Fox. The elections lasted for more than a fortnight, and as the days passed and the voting kept almost even, the partisans threw themselves with frenzied energies into the business of seeking out the more reluctant electors and persuading them to come and register their votes. The Duchess of Devonshire, who on these occasions always took a lodging in Henrietta Street, to be near the scene of operations, and her sister, Lady Duncannon, were staunch Whigs who worked with furious enthusiasm for Fox. 'These ladies being furnished with lists of outlying voters, drove in their carriages to their respective dwellings, sparing neither entreaties nor promises. In some instances even personal caresses were said to have been permitted in order to prevail on the sulky and inflexible; and there can be no doubt of common mechanics having been conveyed to the hustings by the Duchess in her own coach.'[1]

Fox drew ahead. The Countess of Salisbury began counter-operations on behalf of Wray, but she was too late. Fox, returned with a majority of 235, was victoriously chaired through the streets from Covent Garden to Carlton House.

'All minor interests were swallowed up in this struggle,' wrote an observer,

[1] Sir N. W. Wraxall, quoted in *Old and New London*.

'which held not only the capital, but also the nation, in suspense, while it rendered Covent Garden and its neighbourhood, during three successive weeks, a scene of outrage and even of blood.' Others wrote that 'the vulgar abuse of the candidates from the vilest rabble is not rendered endurable by either wit or good temper'. The indefatigable Duchess of Devonshire, at work by eight o'clock in the morning, canvassed in 'the most blackguard houses in Long Acre'.

Towards the end of the nineteenth century and during the early years of the present century, Covent Garden ceased to be primarily a residential area. The rising tide of the market has crept steadily into the surrounding streets of the main square, and more and more of the fascinating old houses have been taken over as business premises. The congregations of St. Paul's have inevitably dwindled, as has happened in nearly all the churches in the City and the heart of London, which have mainly only a daytime population; but St. Paul's, Covent Garden, so close to the theatres, has always been associated with stage people, and it is as the Actors' Church that it is best-known today.

Succeeding rectors have striven to maintain the Sunday congregations. During the Second World War the Reverend Vincent Howson worked devotedly amongst the market people, keeping in touch with all those who were on active service and becoming the friend of many who remained at home. Today his successor, Prebendary Clarence May, is as active in the organizing of weekly midday services and mid-week communion services, as well as the morning and evening Sunday services, at which the subjects for the sermons are usually chosen from the multitude of current social problems. There are special services for the sick, services for blessing the animals, 'Flower' Sundays and a Christmas bazaar. There is a literary society and also a Church Fellowship, which organizes summer outings for its members.

Congregations are not large, but the Church breathes a spirit of informal and heart-warming friendliness. Strangers are expected to drop in at any time and are welcomed. The grass of the garden, gay with flower beds, is cared for.

Memorial services for great actors and actresses are always held either here or at St. Martin-in-the-Fields, and on the west wall of St Paul's are memorial plaques to a number of famous stage people who have died within the last few years; Edouard Espinosa, Sir Charles B. Cochran, Ivor Novello, Sophie Fedorovitch, Leslie Henson, W. Macqueen-Pope and Bransby Williams.

Ellen Terry's ashes, in a silver casket, rest in the south wall, and nearby is the memorial tablet to Dame May Whitty and her husband, Ben Webster.

C. B. Cochran's memorial plaque bears the quotation from Coriolanus: 'I thank you for your voices, thank you. Your most sweet voices.' What better words could evoke such gay and gentle memories?

Chapter 7
The Market

THE old, walled City of London had four ancient produce markets: Billingsgate, Leadenhall, Smithfield and Spitalfields, all owned by the City Corporation. Of these Spitalfields, the smallest, was the market dealing in fruit and vegetables. There was also, where the Mansion House now stands, the Stocks market, built on the site of one of the city's penal stocks. There are records of the Stocks market, for the sale of fish and meat, as early as the reign of Edward I, and by Henry VIII's time there were, in addition to the butchers' and fishmongers' stalls, 20 covered fruit stalls and stalls for the sale of roots, herbs and flowers.

In the seventeenth century Strype, writing of the Stocks market, said that 'it is converted to a quite contrary use; for instead of fish and flesh sold there before the Fire, are now sold fruits, roots and herbs; for which it is very considerable and much resorted unto, being of note for having the choicest in their kind of all sorts, surpassing all other markets in London.'

When the Mansion House was built in 1759, the old Stocks market was removed to Farringdon Street, but it did not survive the change very well, and with the building of Waterloo Bridge, Surrey and Kent growers, taking advantage of the new direct access to Covent Garden, sent their produce there, in preference to Farringdon market. Farringdon's fortunes dwindled, and by 1874 its wares were described as 'very humble . . . The market for vegetables, in fact, is supplied chiefly from the gardens in the immediate vicinity of London, say within ten or twelve miles' radius, while the fruit comes almost exclusively from Kent. The more important supplies, from distant parts of the country, go to Covent Garden and the Borough.'

Towards the end of the seventeenth century, Sir Edward Hungerford commissioned Sir Christopher Wren to build a fruit and vegetable market on the site of his old home, which had been burnt to the ground. The site, by the river, within easy access of the market gardens of Chelsea, was a good one, and by the saving of road transport charges it might well have proved a serious rival to Covent Garden, but it failed.

The area of Spitalfields developed during the seventeenth century, when the silk-weaving industry was established there by Huguenot refugees who had fled from France after the revocation of the Edict of Nantes. The increased population meant the development of the market, the freehold of which was still held by the City Corporation, and as the suburbs of London spread to the east and the north, throughout the eighteenth and nineteenth centuries, the market became ever larger and more important.

Covent Garden, however, grew even more rapidly, and by 1830 it had spread across the whole three acres of the square. On the southern side was a long, continuous row of single-storey shops. On the east were scattered shops and booths. In the north-western corner were more shops, while in the centre of the square and along the north side was an untidy collection of roofed but open-sided booths and tumbledown sheds, in many of which people lived in varying degrees of squalor. Amongst them were the butchers and bakers and peddlers of illicit gin, supplying the wants of the market people.

The traffic in Covent Garden had always been a problem. The narrow streets where the theatres stood were congested by the sedan chairs and their bearers, during the seventeenth and early eighteenth centuries, and by the long lines of carriages of the later years, while from the early hours of the morning till mid-afternoon the carts and drays of the market people struggled to make their way, with their loads of fruit, flowers and vegetables.

During the eighteenth century, the wealthy residents saw the unsightly market buildings spreading and the cumbersome traffic increasing. They at last protested, lodging a complaint with the Duke of Bedford at the nuisance and inconvenience the traffic was causing and begging him to 'take the favourable occasion that will soon offer, by the expiration of the lease of the Market, to become the happy instrument of reviving the decayed credit of the parish and restoring it to its pristine flourishing state . . .' However, the Duke did nothing of the kind. He ignored the petition. The market remained and continued to spread, while the sorely tried residents gradually moved away and Covent Garden declined in gentility. As the lovely old houses were deserted, some were taken over by the market people, others by disreputable members of London's underworld, who let them fall into a state of almost irremediable disrepair.

By 1813 the market had grown so unwieldy that the current Duke obtained from Parliament an Act for regulating it; but 10 years later this was repealed, with the passing of a new Act 'for the Improvement and Regulation of Covent Garden Market' and the building of the present covered market for the Duke by William Fowler.

The old sheds were now cleared away. In their place Fowler built his market, with its central covered arcade of double-storey shops, intersected by a similar arcade at right-angles, the whole building covering an area of an acre and a half. The entrance, with its arch raised on two granite Tuscan columns and surmounted by a triangular pediment carved with the Bedford coat of arms, matched the church, while the arcade, surrounding all four sides of the market, harmonized with what was left of the piazzas. The Duke was given the right to let the shops, to impose market tolls and to make bye-laws for its good government.

A little later, the Borough market was rebuilt, and then Fowler was commissioned to rebuild Hungerford market; but though the Borough was successful, Hungerford failed again and within a few years had become the site for the new Charing Cross station.

Once the market buildings were up in Covent Garden the tone of the place changed and it became more respectable. For the first few years it drew many visitors, particularly in the early hours of the morning. Not a few were late-night revellers, attracted by the fact that a few of the market taverns, including the Kembles' Head in Bow Street, the White Swan in New Row and the Essex Serpent in King Street (said to have received its strange name when a grass snake wriggled from a box of fruit from Essex and headed for the pub), had a special market licence from five o'clock in the morning till nine o'clock.

The new buildings were reserved for fruit and vegetables, the flower market being held at first in the open space in front of the church and round the entrance to the central arcade. Londoners have always loved flowers. In his *Old and New London* Edward Walford quotes a case of bankruptcy, brought in 1871, in which one individual had spent £353 on flowers in six months, the items including half a guinea for a single moss rose and £150 for lilies of the valley and ferns. The old market women were extraordinarily skilful in making bouquets for the stars of the Opera House and Drury Lane. The pea-shuckers, shelling peas for the big hotel orders, worked with incredible speed; and the other free show of the market was the display of agility by the porters, who could balance on their heads nine or ten baskets, piled one on top of the other, with apparently effortless ease. The pea-shellers have all disappeared now and so have the basket-balancers, for the porters use hand trucks these days; safer, perhaps, for them, but not for the unwary pedestrian who happens to cross their paths while they are in full spate with heavy loads.

When Gye rebuilt the opera house, after the fire of 1856, he planned a Floral Hall as a flower market, to be built up against the south wall of the theatre with its entrance in Bow Street. The Piazza Hotel, which had once been the old Piazza coffee house, was pulled down, and on part of the site there took shape the Floral Hall, like a giant conservatory, with its domed glass roof supported by cast-iron pillars, its central arcade and side-walks. It was 90 feet high, 227 feet long, from Bow Street to its west wall, and 100 feet wide from the market to the wall of the opera house. It was made from materials left over when the Crystal Palace was moved from Hyde Park to Sydenham, after the 1851 exhibition. The Floral Hall was ceremoniously opened in 1860 with a grand Volunteer Ball; but thereafter, for no known reason, it was used not as a flower market, but for promenade concerts and similar entertainments. A wholesale flower market was soon afterwards built in the south-western corner of the market, with its entrance in Wellington Street. The first of its three large halls is now used as an unpacking shed, the second for the sale of cut flowers and the third for the sale of plants.

As early as 1890, people were complaining about the congestion growing each year in the new market. 'We are fully cognisant of the fact that Spitalfields and Farringdon absorb some portion of the trade in vegetables; but Covent Garden is *the* market, *par excellence*,' wrote an angry Victorian in the *City Press*, 'and it is a disgrace to the metropolis to be compelled to rely on the capabilities of a place which, spacious as it may be, is fitted at the very utmost to serve as a market for a town of 60,000 inhabitants.'

He might as well have saved himself the time and trouble of writing all that. The market throve, and nothing could check it. The Russell Street extension was built the same year and the Jubilee market in the year of the old Queen's jubilee. Even these additions were not enough for the growing demands of Covent Garden, though, and today the premises used by the market extend over some thirty acres surrounding the original charter market, into Bow Street, Long Acre, Russell Street, Hart Street, King Street, Tavistock Street and even to Inigo Place, inside the very gates of the churchyard.

Many of the firms now occupying the shops in the arcades and the surrounding streets – Lewis Solomon, T. J. Poupart, Muxworthy, Barnett Emanuel, for example – have been there for several generations, and George Monro Ltd., which opened its doors in the North Row in 1862, celebrated its centenary of market trading a few years ago.

The Bedford family disposed of the market and the trading rights after the First World War, and it came to be run by a company calling itself Covent

Garden Market Ltd., but in 1961 Parliament passed the Covent Garden Market Act, establishing the Covent Garden Market Authority, which took over the running of the market early in 1962. The jurisdiction of the Authority extends over six and a half acres, and it has been charged with the task of improving the existing market facilities or providing better ones.

Covent Garden is today the most important of all the United Kingdom fruit and vegetable markets, and one of the largest in the world, equalling those of New York, Paris and Munich. It is a wholesale market, selling to secondary wholesalers and also to retailers. Many of the firms are brokers, buying from bulk suppliers and selling to smaller suppliers, but some also buy to sell through their own organizations, and others have their own orchards and market gardens, both in the United Kingdom and abroad, for wholesale and retail selling. The market now handles seventy million pounds' worth of fruit and vegetables each year and ten million pounds' worth of flowers and plants. There are 200 firms selling fruit and vegetables on commission or on their own account, 40 growers selling their own produce and over 100 firms selling flowers and plants. About 4,000 men are employed in the market; some 2,000 on the administrative and office side of the work, the rest manual workers, mainly porters of various kinds.

Throughout the night and early morning 1,000 lorries bring the produce to the market each day, from all over the country, and over 3,000 lorries come to take it away.

Two-thirds of the value of the produce handled in the market, representing about half its tonnage, is now imported. Into the London docks it comes, from all over the world – bananas from Jamaica and apricots from South Africa, cranberries from Holland and figs from Italy, lemons from Israel and peanuts from China, dates from Tunis and pistachio nuts from Turkey. Much of it is unloaded into trucks and driven straight to the Floral Hall in Covent Garden, which, after losing its roof once during the war and again during a fire in 1956, shed all its former glory and was turned into the Foreign Fruit market.

In 1928 the City Corporation bought the leasehold of the Spitalfields market, extended the market area to more than five acres and created the London Fruit Exchange, only ten minutes' drive from the docks, where imported fruit, mainly apples, oranges and bananas, are auctioned by sample to some 800 buyers at a time, including fruit merchants from Spitalfields, the Borough and also Covent Garden; but the more exotic and expensive fruits go direct to the Garden from the docks.

The business of the market still grows, and each week the congestion of the traffic and the noise and bustle seem to intensify. The Covent Garden Authority has recommended that the market be moved to a new, 80-acre site at Nine Elms, close to Vauxhall. There is much to be said for the change, though many of the market people do not welcome it. They would have more space. The Authority plans adequate marketing, trading and warehouse accommodation, garages, servicing facilities and parking space for 1,500 cars and 2,300 lorries, and the usual supply of snack bars and restaurants. If Parliament approves the plan, the Authority hopes to open the new market at Nine Elms not later than 1971.

The change, discussed for a century or more, is bound to come in the end, but what will take its place in the old market square, so full of memories, so rich in history? Whatever it is, let it be a worthy successor to the ramshackle but endearing old market, which, for all its blowsiness, has always guarded jealously its most valuable possession, its tradition of quality. This is an attribute associated with so much that has come from the Garden; its music, its literature, its art and its theatre, and one which, though increasingly difficult to preserve, is too rare and precious to lose.

THE PLATES

HAS BUTLER, *HERBALIST & SEEDSMAN. LAVENDER WATER*

*Covent Garden Market, from the south. St. Paul's Church is
the far left, and the Royal Opera House in the right backgroun
The Floral Hall is just in front of it, and the main Mar
building is in the centre.*

St. Paul's Church,
from the Piazza.

Goodwin's Court, which runs between St. Martin's Lane and Bedfordbury.

The Theatre Royal, Drury Lane. The main entrance.

The Arcade, Theatre Royal.

The Auditorium, showing the Royal Box, Theatre Royal.

The Grand Staircase, Theatre Royal.

The Augustus Harris Memorial.

Shakespeare Memorial, Drury Lane.

The Saloon, Theatre
Royal.

*The Rotunda,
Theatre Royal.*

The Retiring Room behind the Royal Box, Theatre Royal.

Doorway in the Piazza, leading to No. 43 King Street, an Inigo Jones house where Sir Kenelm Digby and the Earl of Orford once lived. It has since accommodated an hotel, a music hall, the Savage Club, the National Sporting Club, and an old-established Market trader.

The Royal Opera House.

The Flaxman bas-reliefs, Royal Opera House.

The Auditorium, Royal Opera House.

The Crush Bar, Royal Opera House.

St. Paul's Church, from the east.

St. Paul's Church, from the west.

St. Paul's Church: Grinling Gibbons monument.

St. Paul's Church: the interior.

St. Paul's Church: the Altar.

St. Paul's Church: Ellen Terry monument.

Bow Street Police Station.

The main Market building, known officially as the Dedicated Market.

A salesman in the Market.

The Arcade of the Piazza.

Interior of the Market building.

*The Market
Buildings seen from
the Piazza.*

Morning activity.

Beauty in the Market.

Buyers and sellers.

A porter.

The Floral Hall (used as the Foreign Fruit Market), seen from Bow Street; the Royal Opera House beyond.

A porter 'nutting' a box of produce.

Salesmen.

A nun from a nearby Convent collects unconsidered trifles. The Market traders and porters are careful to see that she finds plenty.

A cold morning.

Market transport: one of the ubiquitous barrows, well laden.

Decorative ironwork of the Foreign Fruit Market.

The central part of the Market building, on the south side.
Note the Bedford arms and motto.

e end of the Market day.

*eeping up around the
v famous Covent Garden
a stall.*

BIBLIOGRAPHY

Armitage, Gilbert	*The History of the Bow Street Runners*	Wishart, 1932
Chancellor, E. Beresford	*Annals of Covent Garden*	Hutchinson, 1930
Dane, Clemence	*London Has A Garden*	Michael Joseph, 1964
Fitzgerald, P.	*Chronicles of Bow Street Police-Office*	Chapman and Hall, 1888
Jacobs, Reginald	*Covent Garden, Its Romance and History*	Simkin, Marshall, 1913
Pepys, Samuel	*Diary*	
Pope, W. Macqueen	*Pillars of Drury Lane*	Hutchinson, 1955
Pope, W. Macqueen	*Theatre Royal, Drury Lane*	W. H. Allen, 1945
Pope-Hennessey, Una	*Charles Dickens*	Chatto and Windus, 1945
Rosenthal, Harold	*Two Centuries of Opera at Covent Garden*	Putnam, 1958
Timbs, John	*Clubs and Club Life of London*	Hotten, 1873
Timbs, John	*The Romance of London*	Warne, 1872
Trevelyan, G. M.	*English Social History*	Longmans, Green, 1944
Turner, Clifford	*The Stage As A Career*	Museum Press, 1963
Tute, Warren	*The Grey Top Hat*	Cassell, 1961
Walford, Edward	*Old and New London*	Cassell, 1890
Encyclopaedia of English Literature		Chambers.

Selected Index

This book has been set in Bembo, printed in Great Britain on coated paper by The Grange Press of Southwick, Sussex and bound by Nevett, Key & Whiting Ltd. of Colindale, London.